**Resource Pack 2**

# Community development work skills

Written by

**Dr Val Harris**

# Contents

Community Development Work Skills • **Contents**
*Federation for Community Development Learning*

## Note

To aid your use of this material, pages intended as Tutor Prompt Sheets, Worksheets, Handouts, Case Studies or Reflective Journals have been given an appropriate mark in the top right-hand corners, as shown below.

# Introduction

This resource pack has been produced by the Federation for Community Development Learning as part of its ongoing commitment to develop and share community development learning practice. The pack is part of a series which is linked to the Open College Network Community Development Programme (see www.fcdl.org.uk or www.syocn.org.uk ).

The Programme was developed out of an initial set of courses run by Salford Council for Voluntary Service as part of its community work training programme. The courses were rewritten by Salford CVS and Dr. Val Harris in order to map them to the revised National Occupational Standards for Community Development Work (see www.fcdl.org.uk or www.paulo.org.uk). The Salford units became the first training courses to be mapped to the revised standards in 2002.

The Federation, working with the co-operation of Salford CVS, has accredited the programme through South Yorkshire Open College Network. It has been designed so that further units may be included as and when appropriate. A subsequent set of units has been added to the original list and will be accredited through the OCN Community Development Programme.

The Federation has worked with the Open College Network to develop a National Community Development Award based on this programme. This is the first national community development award that uses the OCN process. It adds to the growing number of qualifications and progression routes for community development workers, managers and activists. For further information on the national award, please contact the Federation or NOCN (www.nocn.org.uk).

## A full programme

This resource pack relates to one of the units in the OCN Community Development Programme and can be used to form part of the national award. The programme covers training courses and materials for a range of qualifications levels. To date, these include foundation (1), intermediate (2) and advanced (3) levels. For further information, see the Get Accredited publication produced by the Federation and OCN.

The programme has been endorsed by the England Standards Board for Community Development Work Training and Qualifications. Additional units will continue to be developed and added to the programme.

The full set of units (to be accompanied by resource packs) is listed on the next page.

### Level 1

1. Understanding community development work
2. Community development work skills
3. Reflective practice.

### Level 2

1. Understanding community development work
2. Community development work skills
3. Effective partnership working
4. Monitoring and evaluation
5. Funding and resources
6. Publicity skills
7. Involving people in community development
8. Planning for community groups
9. Group work skills
10. Developing community organisations
11. Reflective practice
12. Social Justice
13. Identifying needs

14. Neighbourhood regeneration
15. Representing a community of interest/identity
16. Principles into practice.

### Level 3

1. Effective partnership working
2. Monitoring and evaluation
3. Funding and resources
4. Publicity skills
5. Involving people in community development
6. Planning for community groups
7. Group work skills
8. Developing community organisations
9. Reflective practice
10. Social Justice
11. Identifying needs
12. Neighbourhood regeneration
13. Representing a community of interest/identity
14. Principles into practice.

## Using the resource pack

The packs are written in six blocks of 2-hour sessions so that training sessions can be organised flexibly to meet the needs of participants. They are designed to be run with crêches, in evenings, to fit school times etc., and the 2-hour blocks can be added together.

For each four hours of learning there is one learning outcome so that these blocks can be run as stand alone sessions and people can slowly build up their portfolios if they want to. There are learning journal questions, worksheets, etc., to enable participants to gather evidence of their learning from each session.

Each 2-hour session contains:

◆ A detailed session plan
◆ Tutor prompt sheets
◆ Handouts
◆ Exercises, including case studies, work sheets, role plays, stories and games to support each session.

The pack includes everything you need to run the sessions, however, the materials can be adapted and changed to meet both the trainer's style and the needs of participants. The case studies and other exercises might not be relevant to the participants but do give an example which can be adapted by the trainer.

## Developing new resources

The Federation welcomes any feedback and ideas for exercises for the next reprint. This resource pack forms part of a series of publications around community development learning produced by the Federation. For further information, please contact the Federation on 0114 273 9391 or info@fcdl.org.uk

Unit title(s): **Community Development Work Skills**

**Credit value:** One    **Level:** One

| Learning Outcome<br><br>**The learner will be able to:** | Assessment criteria<br><br>**The learner has achieved the outcome because s/he can:** | Evidence Number | Assessor | Moderator |
|---|---|---|---|---|
| 1. Demonstrate their understanding of ways to gather information about a community | 1.1 Give three examples of sources of information about a community | | | |
| 2. Demonstrate an understanding of the roles people take in groups | 2.1 State some of the formal and informal roles people take in groups | | | |
| 3. Demonstrate their understanding of the importance of communications within groups | 3.1 Give two examples of problems that can be caused by poor communication within groups.<br>3.2 Give three examples of the positives outcomes of good communication | | | |
| 4. Demonstrate their understanding of inclusion and exclusion within communities | 4.1 Give two examples of how people can be excluded from community activities<br>4.2 Explain how a community group can include people | | | |
| 5. Demonstrate an understanding of planning as a group | 5.1 State the importance of planning a community group's activities<br>5.2 Give an example of how a group can plan together | | | |
| 6. Demonstrate an understanding of the resources available to a community group | 6.1 Give two examples of support and resources available to a community group | | | |

# Evidence matrix

# Evidence matrix

Unit title(s): **Community Development Work Skills**

**Credit value:** One     **Level:** Two

| Learning Outcome<br><br>The learner will be able to: | Assessment criteria<br><br>The learner has achieved the outcome because s/he can: | Evidence Number | Assessor | Moderator |
|---|---|---|---|---|
| 1. Demonstrate their understanding of the relevance of gathering information about a community and appropriate approaches to use | 1.1 Explain the reasons for gathering information about a community<br>1.2 Describe ways of gathering information about a community | | | |
| 2. Demonstrate an understanding of the roles that people need to take in groups | 2.1 Describe roles within a particular group<br>2.2 Reflect on these roles, including their own role<br>2.3 Identify where power lies in a group | | | |
| 3. Demonstrate their understanding of the way groups develop and the role of communications within groups | 3.1 Describe the life cycle of a group<br>3.2 Describe how communication can create problems within a group.<br>3.3 Give examples of how good communication can aid a group | | | |
| 4. Demonstrate their understanding of inclusion and exclusion within communities | 4.1 Discuss the issues around inclusion and exclusion within their community<br>4.2 Describe how a community group can work more inclusively | | | |
| 5. Demonstrate an understanding of the importance of planning and prioritising in community groups | 5.1 Describe ways of getting a group to prioritise their work<br>5.2 Describe ways of getting a group to produce their own plan | | | |
| 6. Demonstrate an understanding of the resources available to support community development activities | 6.1 Describe the range of support and resources available to community groups and how to access them | | | |

**Session Plan 1 and 2**

# Community development work skills; understanding your community

# Community development work skills; understanding your community

# Session Plan 1 and 2

◆ **Target audience**

Community activists; people working with communities

◆ **Length of session**

2 x 2-hour sessions; four hours in total

◆ **Session aim(s)**

- To introduce the range of skills needed by people working within and with communities

- To examine one key role of collecting information about a community

◆ **Session outcomes**

At the end of the session students/trainees will...

- Demonstrate their understanding of the relevance of gathering information about a community and appropriate approaches to use.

◆ **Indicative content**

- The importance of knowing the communities you are within

- The importance of gathering information; a basic introduction to community profiling

- Deciding what information to gather and where to get it from

- Gathering information in different ways and from different sources

- Making sense of the information gathered and being able to use it and help others to use it

- Presenting information in different ways

- Confidentiality and sensitive issues

# Detailed Session Plan 1

| Time | Content | Exercise/Method | Resources | Notes *core topic or optional if time* |
|------|---------|-----------------|-----------|----------------------------------------|
| 0.00 | Welcome and introduction Domestics | | Tutor Info Sheet: List of domestics | |
| 0.05 | How is your partner? | In pairs make each other a name badge depicting how they feel at this point in time | Tutor Prompt Sheet 1 | |
| 0.20 | Introduction to the aims of the course and OCN accreditation | Tutor input | Tutor Prompt Sheet 2 | Need OCN forms etc; allow longer if this is the first of all accredited courses and you need to explain levels, etc |
| 0.30 | Ground rules | If this is a continuation course then use existing agreed ones, or adapt the standard ones in pack | Standard set of ground rules; flip charted | If a new course then time needed to agree ground rules and timings need to change |
| 0.45 | Overview of skills needed to be a community development worker | Tutor input using the key roles | Handout 1 – Key roles diagram and list | |
| 0.55 | Getting to know a community | Tutor input on key roles Starting with Key Role A – developing working relationships with communities and organisations. Tutor to introduce importance of knowing about communities and to explain about profiles | Handout 2 on profiles | |

# Detailed Session Plan 1

| Time | Content | Exercise/Method | Resources | Notes |
|------|---------|-----------------|-----------|-------|
| | | | | *core topic or* |
| | | | | *optional if time* |
| 1.05 | What information do people need?<br>a) when they move into an area as a resident<br>b) when they go to work as a community development worker in a new area | Introduced by tutor explaining purpose is to think about what information we need to have. Give out Worksheet 1 and split into small groups and ask them to complete both questions.<br><br>Feedback taken from groups on a) complete flip chart with both columns to form a check list.<br>Feedback on b) to get out the information they would need to now and what would be useful | Worksheet 1<br>Tutor Prompt Sheet 3<br><br><br>Need flip chart with columns; one for each question with the same headings as worksheet | |
| 1.35 | Who has information we need | Tutor input on the amount of information that exists; explaining that profiling is about finding out what we can use that already exists and then what else we need to gather.<br><br>Worksheet 2; small groups to think about who can give them information about their area/community. Put onto post-it notes and feedback onto the flip chart to produce categories | Tutor Prompt Sheet 4<br><br><br><br>Worksheet 2<br>Feedback by putting up another flip chart along side results of b) above. Asking groups to put their post-it notes against the different sets of information needed | |
| 2.00 | Ending | | | |

# Domestic checklist

◆ Tell people about:

 1. Fire exits and procedures; and if people leave early they should let tutors know so that the register can be amended

 2. Toilets

 3. Break times and where refreshments are served

 4. Smoking areas

◆ Give out any forms

◆ Remember to make a notice for the door.

# How is your partner feeling?

## Aim

◆ To introduce people to the group, and to check out how they are feeling

## Materials

◆ Post-it notes and pens

## Time

◆ 15 – 20 minutes

## What to do

◆ Give everyone a large post-it notes, and ask them to get into pairs

◆ They ask each other how they feel, and then draw their partner's mood e.g. a stick person lying on a bed with lots of zzz's for a sleepy person

◆ When everyone has done a drawing they introduce their partner to the group, saying 'This is x and they are feeling … today'

◆ Present their partner with their post-it notes to wear.

## Used with

◆ All groups – better on a second session

## Comments

◆ Remind people it is not a drawing competition; bubbles, stick people, etc., are fine

# Aims of the course

**This course aims to give participants an understanding of the range of skills needed to be an effective community development worker, and the opportunity to develop these skills.**

These include:

◆ Gathering information about the communities they are working with and within

◆ Understanding groups and how they work

◆ Tackling exclusions and working to promote inclusion

◆ Setting priorities and planning

◆ Identifying resources.

# Standard ground rules

Make a poster with the following points on, read it out at the beginning and check if anyone needs anything else.

## Way of working together

◆ We will keep to the start and finish times and the times set by the trainer

◆ All mobile phones to be switched off during the session
(emergency tel no for the centre is ............................................ )

◆ We will respect each other and our different views. We will take care not to offend others by our language and/or behaviour

◆ We will listen carefully to each other and allow people to finish. We will try not to hog the conversation

◆ We will keep personal and organisational information confidential to the group

◆ We can ask for clarification about comments/instructions if necessary.

# Key roles of community development work

**A** Develop working relationships with communities and organisations

**B** Encourage people to work with and learn from each other

**C** Work with people in communities to plan for change and take collective action

**D** Work with people in communities to develop and use frameworks for evaluation

**E** Develop community organisations

**F** Reflect and develop own practice and role.

# Key roles of community development work processes

The Reflective Community Development Practitioner

values

practice principles

Key Role A — Develop working relationships with communities and organisations

Key Role B — Encourage People to Work with and Learn from Each Other

Key Role C — Work with People in Communities to plan for Change and Take Collective Action

Key Role D — Work with People in Communities to Develop and Use Frameworks for Evaluation

Key Role E — Develop Community Organisations

Key Role F — Reflect on and Develop Own Practice and Role

Community Development Work Skills • **Session One**
*Federation for Community Development Learning*

# Community Profiles: what are they?

Martin Hawtin

Needs assessments, social audits and community profiles are terms that are often used interchangeably for a similar process. The broadest of these terms is community profiling.

Community profiling has been defined as:

> *A comprehensive description of the needs of a population that is defined, or defines itself, as a community, and the resources that exist within that community, carried out with the active involvement of the community itself, for the purpose of developing an action plan or other means of improving the quality of life of the community.*

Hawtin et al. 1994

The concept of need is complex – who defines it?

◆ The residents themselves?

◆ Members of community groups?

◆ Voluntary organisations?

◆ Local politicians who allocate scarce resources?

◆ National government with its target areas defined by 'multiple deprivation'?

◆ Managers who ration access to resources?

◆ Professionals trained to identify need?

◆ Regional development agencies?

Also, some groups may well have needs that others do not; such as those with religious or disability needs. (See Percy-Smith, J. 1996, *Needs assessment in Public Policy*, Open University Press, Buckingham)

The notion of 'community' also means different things to different people. Here we may refer to a community either as

◆ A geographic area, such as a ward, an estate, a neighbourhood, or administrative area e.g. a school catchment area; or

◆ A group of people with a collective identity, shared interests or needs. This may be based on demographic factors, such as women, minority ethnic groups, children, older people, disabled people, or those with other common bonds such as leisure interests, environmental concerns or members of a religious or political organisation.

# Information people need to live and work in an area

**Split the main group into smaller groups and give out Worksheet 1.**
**Give some examples if they are needed to get people going, and they can also be used as prompts for the feedback:**

- Health services – doctors, dentists, clinics, chemists
- Education services if they have children
- Play groups/nurseries
- Youth clubs
- Evening/day adult education classes/training
- Council information points
- Libraries
- Markets
- Supermarkets
- Banks
- Post offices
- Post boxes
- Refuse collection systems and days
- Resident parking permits

- Parks, open spaces
- Bus services, stops, fares
- Community groups
- Community centres
- Campaigning groups
- Neighbourhood watch
- Churches, mosques, temples, synagogues, chapels
- Outdoor play provision
- Older people's services
- Access buses and where they go
- Late opening chemists
- Hole in the wall cash machines
- Pubs, clubs, social centres
- Type of communities in the area.

# Getting to know an area

In small groups answer the following questions:

1. **When you move into a new area to live**

   ◆ What information would you need to know?

   ◆ How would you get it?

| Information you need | How to get it |
|---|---|
|  |  |

2. **If you were a community development worker moving to a new area:**

◆  What would you need to know?

◆  What kind of information about the new area would be useful?

| *What would you need to know* | *What information would be useful* |
|---|---|
|  |  |

# Existing types of information

- Small area statistics

- Employment/unemployment data

- Surveys

- Grants application forms

- Business plans

- Service monitoring information

- Local directories and resource packs

- Regional development agency information

- Local strategic plans

- Local area plans

- Internet for local council, i.e. yourtown.gov.uk

# Getting information

Look at the list of information a community development worker needs and would find useful. Make a list of who (individuals and organisations) could give you this information.

| Information needed | Where to get it from |
| --- | --- |
|  |  |

Transfer your main points onto post-it notes and be ready in the feedback to place them on the main flip chart against the appropriate heading.

# Detailed Session Plan 2

| Time | Content | Exercise/Method | Resources | Notes core topic or optional if time |
|------|---------|-----------------|-----------|---------------------------------------|
| 0.00 | Wake up game | | | |
| 0.10 | The components and process of a profile | Tutor input – using Handout 2 (from Session 1); group discussion; give ideas about methods and suitability | Tutor Prompt Sheet 5<br>Handout 3<br>Handout 4<br>Flip charts<br>Prepared flipchart on process | |
| 0.20 | Planning a profile | Case study work in small groups | Case studies and Worksheet 3 | |
| 1.20 | Presentations of profiles | Each group has five minutes to outline their plan and then time to answer questions | Tutor to facilitate discussion | |
| 1.50 | Ending game<br>Learning journal questions | | Handout 5 and Reflective journal 1<br>Learning journal questions | |
| 2.00 | End | | | |

# Undertaking a profile

**Explain what a community profile is and link this back to the earlier session on gathering information in order to work in the community. You might find it useful to write out the key points about the process of a profile on a flip chart based on Handout 2.**

The key points that need to be emphasised are that it is about involving people from the community from the beginning, and that in itself it can be an effective way of bringing people together. That all good profiles are quite focused about what they want to achieve and do not try to cover everything. It is important to build on what information already exists and then to look at the most effective ways to fill in gaps. Profiles should be planned from the beginning with their intended audience in mind – whether that is local people or funders – as that will affect their scope and appropriate methods and how the findings will be presented. All of these will be affected by the resources available to carry out the profile.

Use Handout 3 to explain the range of methods that can be used and say that this is not an exhaustive list and they may have other suggestions. It might help the group if you give some examples of which ones may be suitable for what kind of profile, e.g. focus groups for specific problems such as drugs; street survey about parking problems.

Use the following list to explain some of the different ways to present information:

◆ Written in a report

◆ Wall chart

◆ Video

◆ Exhibition

◆ Drama production

◆ Pictures/photos

◆ Wall murals

◆ Web pages

◆ Photography.

# How do you undertake a community profile?

Murray Hawtin

 **Be clear why you are doing it**

For the profile to be effective it is necessary to be clear about the reasons for undertaking it. These may include:

◆ To assess local needs, or to consider people's views and aspirations, in order to contribute to policy making, resource allocation, monitoring and evaluation, or improve service delivery (e.g. neighbourhood renewal)

◆ To initiate a campaign in an area where the existence of unmet need or inadequate resources needs to be demonstrated (e.g. for a community action campaign to provide services)

◆ To make a funding bid requiring information on a community (e.g. to the local authority, lottery or European funding)

◆ To establish baseline information against which future developments can be measured – you need to know your starting point before you can say anything has changed. (e.g. where monitoring is a criterion of funding)

◆ To pursue a community profile project as part of a broader community development strategy, i.e. 'getting to know the area', in which case the process will be as important as the outcome. (community development workers have used this technique for decades).

Community profiles give individuals, or a group of people, the opportunity to express their needs. They seek out the voice of people who are not normally listened to and who may be excluded. They should aim to avoid assumptions made by traditional decision-making based more on conjecture and stereotypes. They achieve this through their content, the way they are undertaken and how people are involved in the process.

# ② The stages in planning a profile

You need to think through quite a lot before you start the profile otherwise you can be gathering too much of the wrong type of information.

## The content

This may either cover the whole range of relevant policy areas i.e. health, housing, education, employment, transport, the environment, etc., or focus on just one or two key issues. The source of the information that goes into the profile may rely solely on **existing data** (e.g. taken from the Census, health statistics, labour market statistics and reports compiled for other purposes by statutory or voluntary agencies), or **new data** collected specifically for this purpose (e.g. through surveys, interviews, group work, public meetings).

So decide what area/topic you want the profile to cover.

## The process

A community profile may be undertaken in a number of ways. To be effective and influential, however, the methods used need to be thorough and well thought out. An ideal process for undertaking a profile may involve all the following steps (although in practice the procedure will change somewhat according to funding and other circumstances):

◆ **Preparing the ground:** Establish a steering group with local residents or members of a community of interest and identity; initial planning; make contacts; learn from others' experiences; identify resources; develop a management structure. (Professional researchers or consultants may be engaged for all or part of the process)

◆ **Setting aims and objectives:** These should be agreed with all involved and stated clearly and based on overall purpose of the profile

◆ **Deciding on methods:** These need to be chosen to suit the objectives, they should be flexible and include gathering primary as well as secondary data. Postal or door-to-door surveys are usually used as the main methods, often supplemented by in-depth interviews of key people and possibly resident focus groups

◆ **Fieldwork:** Produce information-gathering tools, e.g. questionnaires; train those going to be involved in data collection so people are clear what they are asking and how to ask; collect existing and 'new' information; record and analyse the information as it is gathered

◆ **Reporting:** Write up fieldwork, produce, consult and amend draft profile; produce final community profile; disseminate research findings. It might be presented as a written report, an exhibition, a video, an oral presentation etc.

◆ **Action:** Consult over key issues, priorities, action to be taken; draft community action plan.

## ② Community involvement

The nature and level of resident and community involvement will be determined by the type of project. Although a community profile may be undertaken with minimal community involvement, the results will be better and more accurate, and any subsequent decisions more relevant, the greater the level of involvement. Residents and members of different communities should be involved in every stage and level from managing to undertaking the work. There is, potentially, no limit to the number of residents who can become involved, other than the practicalities of group decision making.

It is also useful to include people from different agencies and organisations as well as members of the community. Such representatives may include the statutory services (such as housing, social services, police, library, schools etc.); community and voluntary organisations (such as community development workers, tenants' or residents' group and other local special interest groups); and community representatives e.g. ward councillors, MPs, as religious leaders.

## Resources needed

Community profiling projects require certain resources – depending on the objectives, scale of the project and methods chosen. Although not all are essential, those needed may include:

◆ person power (including local volunteers and staff from agencies). In addition to managing and producing the profile, skills needed may include research design, computing, interviewing skills

◆ Money

◆ Computer

◆ Photocopier

◆ Access to information

◆ Maps

◆ Local contacts and good will

◆ Funding to produce and share the results.

Each profiling project needs to consider whether the resources are already available; if not, are they vital to the project; and, if so, where can they be obtained. This needs to be thought about before the profile is started, otherwise you can get half way through and find you have run out of resources to finish.

# Methods for gathering information

**There are many different methods for gathering information; the choice will be determined by what you want to find out and who you will involve in finding out:**

- Door to door interviews
- Questionnaires to each family
- Street survey
- Public meetings
- Focus groups
- Survey of existing organisations and talking to their staff
- Profiling of key individuals in the community
- Networks and alliances within and between communities
- Survey of statutory agencies
- Making a video of an issue/area
- Running open days
- Listening surveys (meetings with no agendas – just to listen)

- Running street meetings
- Community mapping (making a visual and interactive map)
- Making a directory and resource guide
- Making a model of an area and inviting comments
- Surveys and reports already carried out by other people
- Information collected for funding bids
- Organisations' business plans
- Local, regional and national government data which is already collected and produced for small areas and communities
- Web sites of local area statistics www.irr.org.uk/statistics/employment.html
- Community statistics projects.

# Case studies for community profiling

**1** You have been asked to undertake a profile on the needs of young people (aged 14 – 18) and the facilities available to them. The request has come from the local partnership who are concerned about the lack of young people being involved in the renewal process. They also know that local people are complaining about young people gathering in certain parts of the area in the evenings and at weekends.

**2** A community group has been campaigning to bring a local mill building back to life. They succeed in getting a developer to take it over, to change the mill into flats and small business units. The group are offered the ground floor as a community space. They ask you to undertake a community profile to see what activities they could put on in this space to meet local needs.

**3** A small number of Disabled people get together to try and set up a centre for independent living, where Disabled people can come for advice and support in living independently in the community. They want to know what services Disabled people would want to see in such a centre and to work with existing organisations of Disabled people to gain their support. They ask you to help them design the process for this profile.

**4** A new healthy living initiative is being developed in the area with the aim of improving the health of the people living there. It is a very mixed area and has a poor health record – with high levels of, for example, diabetes, heart disease and obesity. You are employed as the development team and asked to undertake a health profile which will form the basis of an action plan for the project.

# Planning a community profile

Select a case study and discuss how you would plan a profile to obtain the necessary information. You can use the headings below to guide your discussions.

**1** What is the aim of the profile?

**2** Who is the profile aimed at?

**3** Who needs to be involved in the profile?

**4** What information do you need to get?

**5** What information might already exist?

**6** Who can give you the other information?

**7** What resources do you have to support the profile (people, money, etc.)?

**8** What methods would be best to get the information?

**9** What are the issues you need to think about (e.g. confidentiality)

**10** How will you go about collating and analysing the information you gather?

**11** How will you present the profile – what format?

**12** Other notes.

# Further reading, useful addresses

Burton, P. (1993) *Community Profiling: A guide to identifying local needs.* University of Bristol.

Hawtin, M., Hughes, G., Percy-Smith, J. (1994) *Community Profiling: auditing social needs.* Buckingham: Open University Press.

New Economics Foundation  *21 ways to Engage people.*

New Economics Foundation  *Participation Works.*

Henderson and Thomas (1980) *Skills in Neighbourhood Work.*

Percy-Smith, J. (ed.) (1996) *Needs Assessments in Public Policy.* Buckingham: Open University Press.

Save the Children (1996) *Community Profile Resource Pack Guide.* Glasgow: Caledonian University and Save the Children, Glasgow.

*COMPASS for Windows* is a software package for community profiling designed by The Policy Research Institute. It brings together the main elements of primary research to form an integrated, user-friendly, affordable software package enabling community and voluntary organisations and other agencies to conduct social audits or community profiles in their local areas. It covers questionnaire design, data processing and data analysis:

● *For further information, demo version, or order form please contact: COMPASS. Enquiries on 0113 283 1747 or email compass@lmu.ac.uk*

# Reflective Journal

*To be completed after each 4 hours of group work*

Name of participant _____

Name of Tutor/s _____

**1** Give a brief description of the topics covered by the group work and highlight your main areas of learning.

**2** What did you think and feel about the group? What did you contribute to the group and its work?

**3** Did you find anything difficult in the session and/or are there areas you would like us to cover again?

## Portfolio question

**How would you explain the purpose of community profiling?**

*For level 1* You should give three examples of where you can obtain information about a community.

*For level 2* You should explain the reasons for gathering information about a community, and describe, with examples, ways of gathering information about a community.

*(Complete during the week)*

Make notes of anything or thoughts that have occurred during the week which you feel challenged you, or re-emphasised your beliefs/experiences.

Tutor's comments

Signature of participant _____

Signature of tutor/s _____ Date _____

# Groups – how they work and the roles people can take in them

# Groups – how they work and the roles people can take in them

# Session Plan 3 and 4

◆ Target audience

Community activists; people working with communities

◆ Length of session

2 x 2-hour sessions; four hours in total

◆ Session aim(s)

● To explore people's experiences of groups and the roles that people take

◆ Session outcomes

At the end of the session students/trainees will…

● Demonstrate an understanding of the roles that people take in groups.

◆ Indicative content

● Stages in a group's development

● Roles people take in groups

● Allocating roles and responsibilities within a group

● Knowing how you act in a group; roles you might take; how to decide and negotiate your role.

# Detailed Session Plan 3

| Time | Content | Exercise/Method | Resources | Notes *core topic or optional if time* |
|---|---|---|---|---|
| 0.00 | Welcome; admin; collect journals | Tutor input | | |
| 0.05 | Warm-up game | | | |
| 0.15 | Recap ground rules and explain aim of the day | Tutor input | Tutor Prompt Sheet 6 | |
| 0.20 | People's experiences of groups | When it was good it was…. When it was hard it was…. People to put their thoughts onto post-it notes and put onto flip charts | Two flip charts already prepared with headings, Post-it notes | |
| 0.35 | What makes for good and poor group experiences | What makes for good and poor group experiences<br><br>Two groups; one to look at poor experiences, the other at good experiences.<br><br>Feedback to develop a checklist of what makes for a good group | Worksheet 4 | |

# Detailed Session Plan 3

| Time | Content | Exercise/Method | Resources | Notes core topic or optional if time |
|------|---------|-----------------|-----------|-------|
| 0.55 | Understanding the life cycle of groups | Teams to write up ideas about the different stages of a group's life | Tutor Prompt Sheet 7<br>Flip chart on wall or tables with headings | |
| 1.15 | Life cycle of groups | Tutor input to Handout 6; linking this back to the previous exercise | Handout 6 | |
| 1.25 | Skills required for group work | Small groups to think about the skills that community development workers need to work with groups at these different stages.<br>Come back together but no feedback yet | Flipcharts and pens for each group | |
| 1.40 | Task and maintenance roles in groups | Tutor to explain difference between task and maintenacne roles. Take feedback onto prepared flipcharts split into the two headings | Handout 7 | |
| 2.00 | End | | | |

# Introduction to session

**In these next four sessions we will be exploring the second key role – Key Role B which is about encouraging people to work with and learn from each other.**

At this level (level 2) the National Occupational Standards expect people undertaking community development to:

***Contribute to the development of community groups/networks.***

The way that people do this is by:

◆ Helping community groups/networks to identify their strengths and weaknesses

◆ Helping community groups/networks to develop their own practice

◆ Encouraging community groups/networks to work in ways that are inclusive and empowering.

So in the next four 2-hour sessions we will be exploring working together in groups.

# Experiences of groups

Looking at the list made in the previous exercise think about what is behind these experiences.

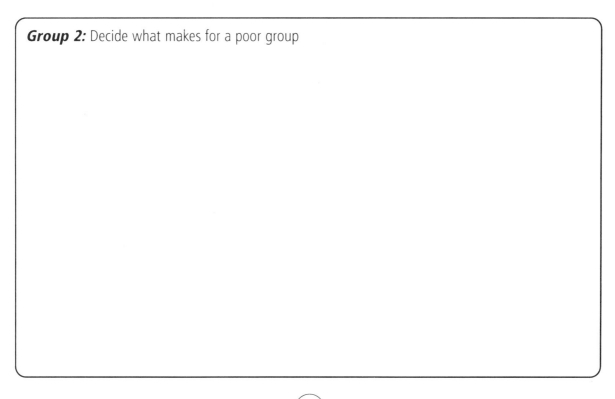

*Group 1:* Decide what makes for a good group

*Group 2:* Decide what makes for a poor group

# The life cycle of groups – exercise

**Split the group into three teams. If you have a group where everyone can move around then pin 3 prepared flip charts on a wall and line the teams up opposite them. If the group are less active then put the flipcharts on tables where people can gather round them.**

Each flip chart should have one of the following headings:

**1** The beginnings of a group (the first few weeks)

**2** The on-going group (after a couple of months or so)

**3** The group that has been going for some time (after several months or so).

If the teams are able to move they line up opposite their flip chart and the front one has a pen. At the signal you give they have to run towards their flipchart and write down any examples or experiences of what might be happening in a group at that stage of its development. They run back and hand the pen onto the next person until it looks like they are struggling to think of new ideas. It is like a relay race and can generate quite a lot of energy and fun.

If the teams are working around a table give them a start signal, and call a halt after a few minutes when each team has had a chance to write down all they can think of.

Ask the groups to sit down and swap around the sheets and add in anything else they can think of.

Sum up these exercises by talking about the way that while groups develop their own patterns, they also tend to go through quite recognisable stages. Use Handout 6.

# The life cycle of groups

**All groups go through different stages as they grow and develop. When it feels heavy going it is worth thinking about where the group has got to in its cycle as that can help you decide what to do and whether you should worry about it.**

◆ People come together because they want to change something and they cannot do it on their own

◆ The group gets together and people want it to work and they assume that everyone is thinking the same

◆ As the group members work together so they find that they have very different expectations of the group and tensions can begin to rise and arguments occur

◆ The group members want to make it work and so try and clarify what the group is there for, there may be competing and conflicting demands on the group

◆ Some people might leave and the others carry on – they are a bit more realistic about what can be achieved, and they start to achieve some of their goals

◆ Conflict surfaces again – it seems hard again and some people just want to give up; it seems hard to achieve anything; people to cling to old ways of working

◆ Suddenly it seems to work again, people go with the flow of the group and there is more energy and the group works well together and begins to achieve again

◆ The group achieves most of its aims and there is a sense that its time has come; people start to think of a life beyond this group; some people leave and a few may move onto other groups or actions; it is a time of celebration and sadness.

This view of groups is that they go up and down – like a roller coaster.

Another model you may have heard of was by Tuckman who had four stages though others added another one at the end:

◆ Forming – coming together

◆ Storming – where the group members are in conflict

◆ Norming – where the group settles down

◆ Performing – where the group works well together

◆ Grieving – where the group comes to an end.

If you join a group that is already working you may find that it is in one of its harder stages and so it will feel like walking into a war zone, or like pulling teeth. It may be worth staying with it for a while as it may just sort itself out and become productive. As a community development worker you need to assess where any group you are working with has got to.

# Task and maintenance roles in a group

Roles in groups can be broken down into two main types:

◆ **Task roles:** those that help get the work done

◆ **Maintenance roles:** those that help to keep the group together.

Both task and maintenance roles contribute to the group achieving what it set out to do. Research has shown that there at least eight main roles in groups.

## Task Roles

**1** **The Initiator** will come up with ideas and start things off – especially useful when the group first gets together. This is often the person who has brought the group together and who may be seen as the 'leader'. It is useful to have initiators in groups, but sometimes they need to be held back a bit!

**2** **The Clarifier** will help people to be clear on what they are saying, and also help the group to see the bigger picture: how what individuals are doing or saying fits in with the group's aims. They may encourage people to be more specific – especially useful if they are taking the minutes.

**3** **The Information Giver** provides information that helps get the task done. This might be 'technical' i.e. facts and figures, or just inside information, such as who's who in the council. At its best the information is relevant and useful, and offered in a sharing way, rather than as coming from the expert on high.

**4** **The Questioner** does just that – asks lots of basic or challenging questions about what the group's doing and why, etc. It's often useful to have someone who can step back from the immediate pressures and be prepared to get back to basics. Such questioning can appear negative, but can be very helpful if it's done in the right spirit.

## Maintenance Roles

**5**    **The Supporter** gives warmth and encouragement to group members. Someone with a warm personality can be a great help to ease tensions and create a good atmosphere.

**6**    **The Joker** provides light relief and an opportunity for the group to let off steam. Beware though that this does not become negative humour with jokes made at the expense of the group's morale and future plans.

**7**    **The Sharer** is someone who brings a more personal angle to what the group is doing, which can be a great help in allowing people to relate more informally and get to know each other. It may be sharing feelings, hopes or fears about group, why they're there and so on.

**8**    **The Group Observer** may comment on how the group is getting on, and in doing so help the group through blocks and tensions. An observer may say things like 'We seem to be getting stuck here' or 'Isn't this a bit competitive?' Done with tact and care it can be a very useful role in the group.

# Detailed Session Plan 4

| Time | Content | Exercise/Method | Resources | Notes core topic or optional if time |
|------|---------|-----------------|-----------|------|
| 0.00 | Wake up game | | | |
| 0.10 | Roles people take in groups – Formal and informal | Pairs to come up with examples of the different roles. Feedback | Tutor Prompt Sheet 8 Flip chart and pens | |
| 0.25 | Roles you take in a group | Analysing your role exercise | Use Worksheet 5 and ask people to think of an example of themselves in a group and complete the box | |
| 0.40 | Allocating roles | Small groups – minimum of five people in each group. Case study of group coming together to achieve a purpose | Case study – part 1 Tutor read out case study | |
| 0.55 | Negotiating a role | Same small groups Case study – part 2 Role play | Case study – part 2 | |
| 1.20 | Accountability of all group members | Same small groups Case study part 3 | Case study – part 3 | |
| 1.35 | Feedback from groups on case study | Key points to be fed back and tutor to lead discussion on issues | | |
| 1.50 | Ending game; return journals | | | |
| 2.00 | End | | | |

# Formal and informal roles taken in groups

**In the previous session we explored the difference between task and maintenance roles that need to be taken in any group. In this exercise we want people to think about the formal roles that people take as well as the informal roles.**

The formal roles can include all the officers' positions if it is a community group. It can be a team leader position within a project or an advisory role undertaken by a community development worker or a consultant.

Ask the participants to work in smaller groups and make lists of all the formal roles they have come across.

Then they should list all the informal roles that they have noticed that contribute to a group being effective, this could be someone who takes on the role to make sure that ideas can be turned into tasks that people can do, or someone who finishes off tasks after an event is over.

# Analysing your own role

Val Harris

**There are a wide range of roles community workers adopt within any group. The actual role you take on will be determined by the stage of the group's development, your skills and experience, and if you are employed, what is acceptable to your employer/management committee.**

We have discussed how groups have a life of their own, so your role will change over time and in relation to its situation. For example, when a group is starting up it will need more help with the basics of how to organise itself. While later on it may need help in recruiting new members or seeking advice on becoming involved in a partnership.

Using the examples overleaf as a guide, you can explore and analyse your role(s) with a group. List 1 gives some of the roles involved in helping a group decide where it is going, while List 2 gives some of the roles involved in building and maintaining a group. There will be many other roles you could take – these are only examples.

Think of a group you work with or are a member of and fill in the box below:

| Roles you do or could take | Purpose of the role | The action(s) you take | Comments on your action(s) | Changes you want to make to your role |
|---|---|---|---|---|
| | | | | |

## List 1: Examples of helping a group to achieve its goals

| Role | Purpose | Action Taken |
|---|---|---|
| **Initiator** | To give direction and purpose to a group | Define problems; propose tasks and goals; suggest procedures and solutions |
| **Information seeker** | To find out what the group knows; encourage the group to seek more information | Request relevant facts |
| **Information giver** | To enable the group to be better informed | Offer relevant facts |
| **Opinion seeker** | To find out individual opinions | Ask for opinions |
| **Opinion/advice giver** | To provide a basis for a group to start to come to a decision | Evaluate and elaborate group members' suggestions |
| **Clarifier** | To reduce confusion | Define terms; interpret ideas; suggest options; spot ambiguities; give examples |
| **Summariser** | To draw ideas together | Repeat and relate statements; link themes; show contradictions; offer solutions |

## List 2: An example of building a group by helping to set its own ground rules

| Role | Purpose | Action Taken |
|---|---|---|
| **Encourager** | To enable others to feel recognised and that they have a contribution to make; to facilitate communication | Be responsive and friendly to others; draw out a silent member; suggest procedures for discussion to allow more people to join in |
| **Commentator** | To call the group's attention to the existence of certain reactions, ideas or suggestions | Restate what others have said |
| **Conciliator** | To relieve tensions and encourage group cohesion | Inject humour; suggest compromises |
| **Benchmarker** | To make the group aware of direction and purpose | Suggest directions and targets; analyse progress towards goals |
| **Interpreter** | To explain, or interpret, what someone else has said | Paraphrase initial speaker |
| **Listener** | Provide stimulating, interested audience for others | Listen and comment constructively |

**NOTE** –*You can take on any of these roles in your more formal role of chair, secretary, fund-raiser, advisor, etc.*

# Deciding of roles within a new group

## The situation

The local community association has been campaigning for some time to get a piece of waste land in the area cleaned up. The land is near sheltered accommodation for older people and is owned by the same Housing Trust. They agree to let the community association take it over on a peppercorn rent and a long lease. The community association decides to set up a new organisation to develop and run the project.

## Part 1

What roles will be needed in such a group? Make a list of both the formal and informal roles that will be needed to get the group going.

| Formal roles | Informal roles |
|---|---|
| | |

How would you go about allocating these roles to people who are interested in the project?

# The scenario continues ...

**The Housing Trust has asked its community development workers to give this new group some assistance.**

In your group you need two people to volunteer to be these community development workers, and the rest of your group take on the role of members of the project group.

**The task is for the project group members** to think about what role(s) they want the community development workers to take on.

[ ]

**The two community development workers** have to think about what roles they can take on in the two days they have been allocated to work with this group.

[ ]

**Allow yourselves 5–10 minutes for thinking time, and then you will role-play the negotiations between the workers and the group members.**

Once the role play is completed (about 10 mins) make a note of the roles that the group will take on and what they have agreed as an appropriate role for the community development worker.

| Roles of the workers | Roles of the group members |
| --- | --- |
|  |  |

# The scenario continues ... agreement on accountability

Once you have decided on the roles that people will take on, you need to draw up an agreement within the group on accountability. This will apply to all members of the group and the community development workers. It will lay out how they will remain accountable to the group in relation to the tasks they take on and the external contacts they make on behalf of the group.

# Reflective Journal

**To be completed after each 4 hours of group work**

Name of participant _____

Name of Tutor/s _____

**1** Give a brief description of the topics covered by the group work and highlight your main areas of learning.

**2** What did you think and feel about the group? What did you contribute to the group and its work?

**3** Did you find anything difficult in the session and/or are there areas you would like us to cover again?

# Portfolio question

*For level 1* You should describe some of the formal and informal roles people can take in groups.

*For level 2* You should describe a particular group and the roles that people take within it. Reflect if these roles are appropriate and comment on your own role. Explain who holds power within the group.

*(Complete during the week)*

Make notes of anything or thoughts that have occurred during the week which you feel challenged you, or re-emphasised your beliefs/experiences.

Tutor's comments

Signature of participant _____

Signature of tutor/s _____ Date _____

Understanding Community Development Work • **Session Four**
*Federation for Community Development Learning*

# Making groups work effectively

# Making groups work effectively
## Session Plan 5 and 6

◆ **Target audience**

Community activists; people working with communities

◆ **Length of session**

2 x 2-hour sessions; four hours in total

◆ **Session aim(s)**

- To explore what goes on within groups and what will make them more effective.

◆ **Session outcomes**

At the end of the session students/trainees will...

- Demonstrate their understanding of the importance of communications within groups.

◆ **Indicative content**

- Group autonomy/self determination
- Communication within a group
- Potential problems in a group and how to handle them
- Dealing with different opinions.

# Detailed Session Plan 5

| Time | Content | Exercise/Method | Resources | Notes *core topic or optional if time* |
|------|---------|-----------------|-----------|----------------------------------------|
| 0.00 | Welcome; admin; collect journals | | | |
| 0.05 | Warm up game | Chinese whispers | Tutor to start a sentence at the beginning of the circle | |
| 0.15 | Aims of the session | Tutor input | Tutor Prompt Sheet 9 | |
| 0.20 | Square wheels – what is going on in this scene | Small groups to say what they think is going on. Whole group to agree the problems. Small groups reconvene to discuss if this was a group, what would improve the situation? Feedback | Square-wheels picture Tutor Prompt Sheet 10 | To raise issues of leadership and blocks to a group getting going |
| 0.55 | Communications within groups | Tutor to pull out issues of communication into two columns – problems created by poor communications; positive outcomes from good communications | Tutor Prompt Sheet 11 | |

# Detailed Session Plan 5

| Time | Content | Exercise/Method | Resources | Notes *core topic or optional if time* |
|------|---------|-----------------|-----------|-------|
| 1.05 | Power within groups | Pairs/trios to use their experience to decide who has power and why? Feedback. Tutor to create a list of power sources | Tutor Prompt Sheet 12 | |
| 1.30 | Impact of power dynamics on communication within groups | Tutor to add in additional comments from feedback on the two types of communication. General discussion on the need for power to be shared more equally | Tutor Prompt Sheet 13 | |
| 1.40 | Fish in the forest | Tutor to tell the story and then to ask the group to consider the power issues involved | Fish in the Forest story. Tutor info sheet | |
| 2.00 | End | | | |

Community Development Work Skills • **Session Five**
*Federation for Community Development Learning*

# Introduction to session

This session relates to aspects of the Key roles B and C in the National Occupational Standards. Tutor Prompt Sheet 6 gave details of Key role B and you can refer back to last week.

*Key role C is about working with people in communities to plan for change and take collective action.*

There are 2 units at this level:

**1** Work within communities to select options and make plans for collective action; this involves:

◆ Contributing to gathering information to aid decision-making

◆ Contributing to evaluating and selecting options for collective action

◆ Contributing to developing a collective plan of action which ensure participation.

**2** Contribute to collective action within a community

◆ Encourage people's participation in collective action

◆ Help a community group put an agreed plan into action.

Community development is based on people working together to bring about desired changes. The aim is to develop strong and independent groups of people who work well together. This will require the group members to develop their skills at working together.

One of the main building blocks of good group working is effective communication between all members. Problems often arise because of poor communication between people. In the next four hours we will be exploring how to develop strong and effective groups and to deal with some of the common problems that can occur.

# Square Wheels

**1** Organise participants into small groups and give them copies of the square wheels picture.

**2** Ask them first to discuss what they think is going on in this picture and what problems they can see.

**3** Bring them back together and get the whole group to agree on what they think is happening.

**4** Ask them to return to their groups and consider that if this scenario was a community group what could improve the situation.

**5** Then ask each group to feed back their ideas to the whole group.

# What's going on?

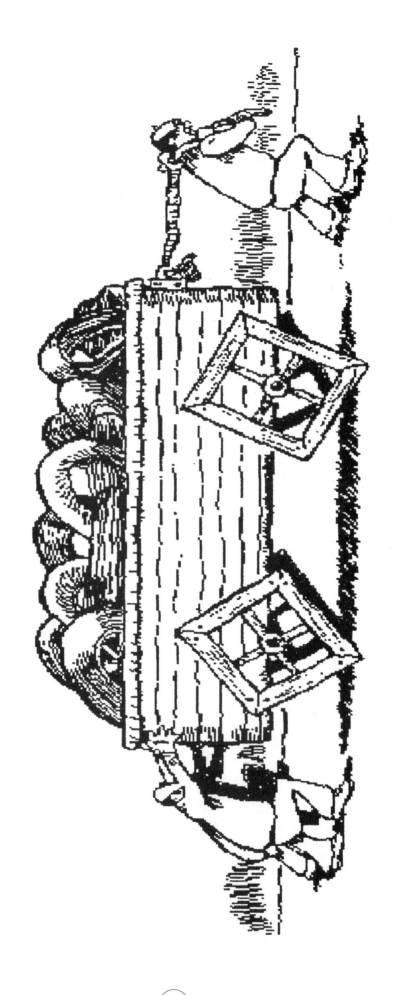

# Good and poor communications

**This exercise is designed to help people gather evidence for their portfolio.**

Divide a flip chart into two columns or use two flipcharts if you have the space. The two headings are:

◆ Problems created by poor communications

◆ Positive outcomes of good communications.

Ask the group to think about the previous exercise and recap on what was helping and what was hindering communication in the square wheels scenario. Then ask them if they can think of any other communication pluses and minuses that you could log here.

Leave the flip charts visible to the group as you will be coming back to them before the end of the session.

# Who has power and why?

**Ask the participants to get into pairs or trios and to think about the groups they are involved in, or have been. If they have been on the Understanding Community Development Course you can remind them of the session on the different sources of power that communities and other organisations have.** (Reference to Handout 9 in that pack)

The task for the pairs/trios is to list the different power sources that people in the group may have. For example:

◆ Confidence to talk in meetings

◆ Being able to think on your feet and respond quickly

◆ As chair they get to control meetings

◆ As secretary they may set the meeting's agenda

◆ As treasurer they have information about money and may be able to baffle people with spreadsheets

◆ Who gets to open the post, may keep information about training courses to themselves

◆ Representatives at other meetings who agree to something on behalf of the group without checking it out

◆ The community development worker who knows what is going on

◆ Advisors/experts who have specialist knowledge which the group needs

◆ The person who organises the group's database on the computer

◆ The fund-raiser

◆ The wheeler-dealer who can get hold of resources.

There will be many more.

Keep the exercise quite short and quick. During the feedback make a checklist from the different ideas which can be used in the next exercise. If the group doesn't come up with any ideas, you may need to suggest some to go into the checklist.

# Types of communication

**In this whole group session you return to the flip charts on communication. Ask the group to consider how the power dynamics they had been discussing could impact on communications within a group.**

Then you can lead a general discussion about the other aspects of power within a group and how sharing power around can create a stronger and more sustainable group. Some of the key points to make are how to avoid a group becoming dependent on one or two people:

◆ That they may get tired and walk away, and the group does not have the skills, contacts or confidence to take over

◆ That other people who are in the group may feel they are not really contributing, that their views are not heard so they may as well not go

◆ That people from outside just think it is just a few people who are concerned about an issue. So they do not take it seriously as they assume it is not a real community issue

◆ That a lot of energy can go into power battles within a group rather than into bringing about the desired change in their community

◆ That other people's skills and expertise will be lost to the group if the leaders do not find a way to enable them to use their skills and contribute their knowledge.

# Fish in the Forest

One day when she was digging up her little bit of land to plant some seeds a woman found a treasure. She took it home and showed it to her partner saying 'look at this, we have been sent a fortune so we must hide it somewhere safe'. Her partner suggested they bury it in their cottage, and so they dug a hole in the floor and buried it. After a while the man went out to meet his friends and the woman worried what he would tell them as she knew he couldn't keep a secret. She felt everyone would know about their luck before long.

So while he was out of the house, the woman dug up the treasure and took it to her secret hiding place in the chicken hut. When her partner returned she said to him; 'Tomorrow I want you to come with me, we are going to the forest to gather fish. The other women tell me there are a lot of fish in the forest. We have only to go and gather them, so we will go tomorrow.' The man laughed 'fish in the forest!' but the woman replied sharply ' the other women have found them there and they told me, so you had better come with me'.

The next day she got up early, and from her larder she took a few fish and a hare and put them in a basket. She hurried off to the bakers' and bought some sweet cakes, put them in her basket and went into the forest. She looked all about to check no one was watching. Carefully she placed the fish amongst some bushes alongside the path. She then hung the cakes from a tree and went to the riverside where she slung the hare onto a fishing hook. She set the line and cast the hare into the water. She then made her way home.

After breakfast she reminded her partner of the planned trip into the forest. They hadn't gone very far when she pointed out some fish lying in the bushes. The man didn't show any surprise, he just picked them up and put them in the basket. Then he noticed the pear tree, which was richly laden with sweet cakes. He loved these cakes and said 'look at these cakes, how strange to find sweet cakes on a pear tree'. The woman answered 'it does happen, I have known this tree to be laden with cakes before now. The women tell me that sometimes the rain brings these cakes, they have seen it as well'. The couple then decided they should return home with all their pickings.

On their way back they passed the small river and the man noticed that there was a fishing line; 'Look at that line, there is no one near it. I am sure something is caught on that line… I cannot believe my eyes…look at that…it's a hare on the line!'

'That's not so unusual' said the woman, 'other women have told me about how their partners catch hares in the river, but as you never go fishing…'

By now the man was becoming quite frightened and didn't like the forest any more. So they went home and made a lovely meal.

Meanwhile the news that the woman had found some treasure had spread across all the village and beyond. Inevitably the landowner heard the rumour and summoned both of them to his castle. He spoke first with the man, and then called in the woman and said 'now you must speak the truth, he has told me everything about you finding a treasure.'

'No, my lord.' replied the woman.

'Now don't try and deceive me, I know you have buried it under the cottage floor'.

'Have mercy, my lord' the woman answered 'my husband does not know what he says, he has been a bit unusual for some time now'.

The man looked outraged, 'I do know what I am saying, I am speaking the truth – you did find a treasure'.

'Well if you are so certain, tell the lord where I found the treasure, when was it?'

The poor man confidently replied 'I remember clearly, it was the day before we found the fish in the forest, there were cakes on the pear tree, it had rained sweet cakes? Remember? and I fished a hare out of the river. True?'

The woman just looked at the lord of the castle as if to say, 'see what I mean'. So he sent them both home and had the cottage floor dug up, but nothing was found. What she did with the treasure is another story.

# Fish in the Forest

**Tell the story of the fish in the forest. Once you have told the story ask the group to think about what was happening in the story – who had what power and how were they using it? You might find it easiest to structure the discussion by looking at each of the characters in turn, the woman, the man, the Lord, the villagers.**

The moral of this story can be described as having to think both about how to plan to respond to something happening and then how to deal with peoples' reactions to the event.

This will lead into the two aspects to be covered in the next session.

# Detailed Session Plan 6

| Time | Content | Exercise/Method | Resources | Notes *core topic or optional if time* |
|------|---------|-----------------|-----------|-------|
| 0.00 | Wake up game | | | |
| 0.10 | Decision-making in groups | Tutor input – recap on previous session; raise issues of decision-making | Tutor Prompt Sheet 14 | |
| 0.15 | Planning an effective group | Small groups to design the structures for a new group to ensure good communication and decision-making. Feedback from each group to say how they would approach the situation | Exercise – designing a new group Tutor Prompt Sheet 15 | |
| 0.50 | Conflict in groups | Tutor input on problems that arise within groups despite the careful planning. Whole group giving examples of behaviour within groups they have found unhelpful. In small groups discuss why they think this might have occurred. Feedback | Tutor Prompt Sheet 16 | |
| 1.15 | Analysing the problem | Six hats; groups to think of a problem in a group and write it up. Pass on to next group to resolve | Handout 9 | |
| 1.50 | Ending game; give out journals | | | |
| 2.00 | End | | | |

# Decision making in groups

Many problems arise from the way that decisions are made, or not, by members of groups. People may feel they have been excluded from the process, that their opinion wasn't heard, or didn't count. Others may think that lots of valuable time was taken up with long discussions about minor decisions which didn't need everyone to be involved in making.

Good group work requires good decision-making. In order for this to happen there needs to be effective structures in place and people willing to work to the agreed structures.

You could give some examples of the decision making process.

◆ **The plop** – someone says something and the idea sinks without trace – like a stone in a pond, so the group makes a decision by not making a decision

◆ **The one-person decision** – where someone makes a decision and expects others to follow, but often finds they are on their own when it comes to carrying it out

◆ **Topic jumping** – just as a group is about to make a decision, someone suggests something else which may or not be relevant, and can stop the group making a decision

◆ **The handclasp** – one person says something, another says 'that's a good idea' and somehow the decision has been made without discussion

◆ **The clique** – a few people get together beforehand to plan what they want. This can be good or bad – sometimes it allows people to be able to get their voices listened to who don't normally get heard

◆ **Minority** – a few people make the decisions but they don't do it consciously, more because they are powerful and can dominate, and then they wonder why other people are apathetic

◆ **Majority vote** – can be effective but watch out for those who are in the minority if they feel they have not been heard

◆ **Silent consensus** – where it is assumed that people have agreed when actually they have not felt able to disagree and so kept silent

◆ **Consensus** – to get an agreement in this way requires compromise or a combination of different possibilities once all the views have been heard. It takes time as it means carefully listening to all the arguments and then trying to come to an agreement as a group.

*Adapted from Training for Transformation,
book 2. 1995 Mambo Press*

# Designing a new group

You went along to your local community centre to find out about the council's plans for your area. You hear that there are plans to let private developers build executive houses on one of the few remaining green spaces. You end up joining with some other local people to form an action group to oppose this idea.

At its first meeting you all have to decide how you will work as a group so that everyone can be involved and the group can make best use of everyone's experiences and skills. You know from past experience of groups in the area that there is a danger that they get taken over by a few vociferous people who think they know what is best for everyone.

**Your task is to decide how you could organise the group so that everyone is able to participate as much or as little as they can, and that power is shared amongst the members.**

You need to make sure that you decide:

◆ How will information be passed around to everyone so that they know what is going on?

◆ How will decisions be made about what actions to take?

◆ Who will take decisions?

◆ How will the action group communicate with the outside world?

# Forming new groups

**Hopefully the small groups will have come up with the key elements for structures that will ensure peoples' involvement and create a strong independent group.**

The key points to pull out are:

◆ The group will need to agree its goal – so time needs to be allowed for this at the beginning

◆ How and where can differences be explored and discussed so that they develop an agreed strategy to achieve their goal?

◆ As an action group they will need to be able to keep everyone up to speed with developments and changes, such as the developers offering to build fewer houses

◆ Communication between the action group and the outside world will be important – for example how will they respond to accusations in the local paper of being NIMBYs (not in my backyard)? Or to the council asking to meet a representative?

◆ How to ensure that people who are available at different times of the day/evening are able to participate

◆ Different kinds of decisions may need to be taken by different people. What decisions require all members to be involved, what can be delegated and how to deal with urgent decisions?

◆ In order to make decisions people need information in a form they can understand.

# Conflict in groups

**Begin by explaining that while planning in advance can help solve some difficulties in groups, other difficulties may arise as the group gets going and develops its own dynamics. Ask the group to come up with some examples of conflict in groups and write them on the flip chart.**

You are going to ask them to work in small groups to think about ways of handling such conflicts. However, first you will give them some ideas of what might be behind such behaviour.

It might be that people:

◆ Feel out of their depth

◆ Have different motivations

◆ Don't feel skilled enough to work in a group

◆ React to change in different ways (avoiding or confronting it)

◆ That they have different ideas of the best strategy to adopt because of their experiences

◆ Have problems back at home

◆ Lack confidence and/or easily feel put down by other members of the group

◆ Etc., etc.

Their task in the small groups is to take some of the conflicts that had been noted on the flipchart and think about what might be behind such behaviour.

This is quite a quick exercise, as you want them to spend more time on the detailed work in the next exercise.

# Six Hats

The six hats technique is a way of analysing problems and situations by separating out the different aspects of a particular situation or problem. It uses creativity and quality thinking in a group and it is a fast method.

How to use the method:

**1** Form into small groups

**2** Decide on a problem that one or more of you is having within your group

**3** Write out the problem on a sheet of flip chart paper in enough detail that someone else can understand it

**4** Pass your sheet onto the next group

**5** Take a sheet from another group

**6** Agree one of you will be the facilitator – they wear the blue hat and their task is to keep you on track

**7** Using the sheet with the hats on it work your way through each hat and make notes on the sheet or a flipchart, so start with the silver hat – what do you know about the situation, what are the facts?

**8** Then move onto the other hats in turn – recording your responses as you go

**9** At the end decide what you would recommend as a solution to the problem. Write it down

**10** Pass the problem, with the steps and your recommendation, back to the originating group

**11** Receive back your original problem sheet and look at what has been suggested and the stages they went through

**12** Discuss in the whole group what you thought of the technique.

# Six Hats Explanations

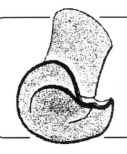 *The blue hat is worn by the facilitator. They take the group through the process and they keep things moving. Facilitators summarise the discussion at times to support the group's thinking.*

 *The silver hat looks at the facts. What do we know about? What is the situation?*

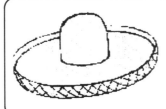 *The yellow hat looks at what is positive in the situation. What is there to build upon?*

 *This is the grey hat – this looks at what is not right with the situation. What bells does it ring from our past experiences?*

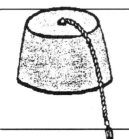 *This is the red hat – this looks at the emotions raised by this situation. How do we feel about it? What are our hunches and intuition?*

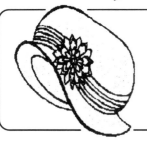 *This is the green hat – this is the creative hat and gets us thinking about what <u>could</u> be. It brings in new ideas, opportunities, resources and alternatives.*

| Hat | Comment |
|---|---|
|  |  |
|  |  |
|  |  |
|  |  |
|  |  |
|  |  |

**Our solution is...**

# Reflective Journal

**To be completed after each 4 hours of group work**

Name of participant _____

Name of Tutor/s _____

**1** Give a brief description of the topics covered by the group work and highlight your main areas of learning.

**2** What did you think and feel about the group? What did you contribute to the group and its work?

**3** Did you find anything difficult in the session and/or are there areas you would like us to cover again?

## Portfolio question

*For level 1* You are demonstrating your understanding of the importance of communications within groups.

You should give two examples of problems that can be caused by poor communication within groups and explain why they were a problem. Then give three examples of good communication which hat had positive outcomes and explain why they were helpful to the group.

*For level 2* You are demonstrating your understanding of the way groups develop and the role of communications within groups.

You need to refer back to some of the work you did in previous sessions and describe the life cycle of a group. You should describe, with examples to illustrate your points, how poor communication can create problems for a group. Then you can give examples of how good communication can help a group achieve its goals.

*(Complete during the week)*

**Make notes of anything or thoughts that have occurred during the week which you feel challenged you, or re-emphasised your beliefs/experiences.**

Tutor's comments

Signature of participant _____

Signature of tutor/s _____ Date _____

# Promoting inclusion and tackling exclusion

# Promoting inclusion and tackling exclusion
## Session Plan 7 and 8

◆ **Target audience**

Community activists; people working with communities

◆ **Length of session**

2 x 2-hour sessions; four hours in total

◆ **Session aim(s)**

- To develop an understanding of the impact of exclusion on communities and individuals and how to develop inclusive groups and communities.

◆ **Session outcomes**

At the end of the session students/trainees will…

- Demonstrate their understanding of inclusion and exclusion within communities.

◆ **Indicative content**

- Working with the powerless/working on the margins

- Relating power and powerlessness to their community (cross reference to Understanding Community Development Work)

- Barriers to involvement by individuals and groups

- Understanding and using networks to make links and contacts

- Working with others; individuals and organisations

- Participation and deciding if you want to participate.

# Detailed Session Plan 7

| Time | Content | Exercise/Method | Resources | Notes *core topic or optional if time* |
|------|---------|-----------------|-----------|------|
| 0.00 | Welcome and admin | Tutor input | | |
| 0.05 | Warm up game | | | |
| 0.15 | Aim of the day | Tutor input on the link to key roles and practice principles | Tutor Prompt Sheet 17 | |
| 0.20 | Why is community development work carried out in areas described as 'deprived' or 'disadvantaged'? | Tutor input and whole group discussion | Tutor Prompt Sheet 18 | |
| 0.35 | Inclusion and exclusion; Understanding the words and their context | Small groups to discuss community exclusion and inclusive groups using worksheet | Tutor Prompt Sheet19 Worksheet 6 | |
| 0.50 | Whose voices are heard and whose not | Pairs to 'map' the voices within their community that are listened to, and those who are not involved, heard or consulted | Tutor Prompt Sheet 20 | |
| 1.10 | Why are some voices not heard? What can community development workers do to help them get their voices heard? | Small groups using material from previous exercise; worksheet. Feedback | Tutor Prompt Sheet 20 Worksheet 7 | |
| 2.00 | End | | | |

# Aim of the session

The aim of the next two sessions is to explore the issues around inclusion and exclusion as it affects communities.

Community development work is based on the ideal that all those within communities who want to can become involved and have a say in how their community should develop.

All of the key roles within the national occupational standards require practitioners to involve people from different communities in the groups and networks that will work to improve the situation in any area or community of interest.

In these sessions on inclusion you will find it helpful to refer to the practice principles and particularly the following points:

**1** Social justice

- ◆ Respecting and valuing diversity and difference

- ◆ Addressing power imbalances

- ◆ Pursuing civil and human rights for all.

**2** Self determination

- ◆ Communities do not have the right to oppress other communities

- ◆ Raising awareness of the choices open to them.

**3** Working and learning together

- ◆ Ensuring all perspectives within the community are considered.

**4** Participation

- ◆ Promoting especially the participation of those traditionally marginalized or excluded

- ◆ Recognising and challenging the barriers to full and effective participation.

# Why carry out community development work?

**The aim of this discussion is to get the group members to think about where community development work is carried out and why. It is the time to introduce some of the current governments' policies and the thinking behind them.**

**The policy examples below are relevant to England. Northern Ireland, Scotland and Wales have similar policy initiatives, for example, Communities First in Wales and Social Inclusion Partnerships in Scotland.**

The points to raise in this discussion are that the government states it is concerned about the inequalities within society between the rich and the poor. It has developed many area-based policies on the premise that the worst areas in England should get the most help from the government. It used the deprivation indices to decide which were the 88 most deprived areas within the country. It started to use these in each policy initiative – for example, New Deal for Communities, Pathfinder Management Programmes, Action Zones (initially for health, education, crime), Community Empowerment Teams, Community Cohesion teams. *(You should chose the ones that are most relevant to the area/group you are training.)*

The government has mainly defined community in terms of geography, or neighbourhoods – hence the Neighbourhood Renewal agenda. The government says it wants to see local people getting involved in its initiatives and taking the lead instead of the professionals. With many of these initiatives there have been jobs created for community development workers, partnership workers, regeneration officers ... most of them with some brief to work with and engage local people and communities.

Ask the group to discuss what they think of these approaches. You may find it helpful to pose questions such as, 'Does this mean that the government thinks that the poor cannot organise themselves?' or 'Is this another way of controlling people?'

The aim of this discussion is to get the group to look behind what might be happening in their local area and to think about the agenda of central, and therefore, regional and local government. It should set the scene to move into the next exercise on inclusion and exclusion and what they mean.

# Inclusion and Exclusion

**Introduce the concepts of inclusion and exclusion by referring to the previous discussion about government policy and how they say they want to create a society where all people can be full members and actively involved. The words inclusion and exclusion have been around for a little while now. Governments use them in nearly all of their policies and funding programmes, and community development workers are expected to develop inclusive groups and communities.**

Using Worksheet 6, organise the participants to work in small groups. Ask them to examine:

**1** What communities may be excluded from?

**2** What an inclusive group/ network might look like?

Obtain feedback on question 1 first, to get the bigger picture of exclusion acting at a societal level, of how communities can be excluded and some of the reasons for this.

Then get feedback on question 2 to explore how groups and networks can include/exclude people – either as individuals or as communities of interest/identity.

Sum up by recognising that any neighbourhood or community of interest will have many competing and possibly conflicting groups within them, and not everyone can agree. We need to recognise differences and be prepared to listen and negotiate at all times.

# Inclusion and Exclusion

In your group discuss the following questions and make notes to feed back.

*1. What do you think the word 'exclusion' means when applied to your communities? What are they excluded from?*

*2. If a community group/network described itself as 'inclusive' what would you expect to find it was doing?*

# Mapping whose voices are heard and whose are not

**This exercise aims to help participants to think about their community and who is currently heard or listened to. Then to think about those who are not involved, not heard or consulted.**

Ask people to work in pairs – ideally those involved in the same community group or network, or with similar ones. They are to draw a circle in the centre to represent their community and then draw several concentric rings (like an onion or dartboard) around the central point. People should write in the rings nearest the centre those who have the most influence and who are actively involved. Those with less involvement should be written in the rings further away.

Around the edge they should write on post-it notes all those groups/communities of interest they know who exist in their community but who are not listed.

Feedback by putting their maps on the walls for people to look at whilst the tutor collects the post-it notes and groups them onto a flip chart sheet. Summarise by looking at all the maps of people who are seen as included.

Return to the flipchart with those who have not been included. Put the participants into small groups by merging the pairs into fours. Give each group a number of the post-it notes relating to one or more excluded group and ask them to complete Worksheet 7. This asks them to consider why those particular group(s) are not being heard, and then what can community development workers do to help them get their voices heard.

You may need to give some examples of why people's voices are not heard – attitudes of others, lack of economic power, cultural factors, discrimination, perceptions of being awkward or compliant, social standing or lack of, etc.

Feedback by asking each group to talk in turn and asking other groups to comment.

# Voices: who is heard?

You will have been given one or more groups of people who are often excluded or marginalised. Discuss the following two questions and make your notes ready to feed back to the whole group.

*What group(s) did you have to discuss?* ................................................................

*1. Why do you think this group/these groups find it hard to get their voices heard?*

*2. As community development workers what can you suggest can be done to get their voices heard?*

Community Development Work Skills • **Session Seven**
*Federation for Community Development Learning*

# Detailed Session Plan 8

| Time | Content | Exercise/Method | Resources | Notes core topic or optional if time |
|------|---------|-----------------|-----------|---------------------------------------|
| 0.00 | Wake up exercise | | | |
| 0.10 | Making contact with marginalised communities | Tutor input<br>Two groups – Case studies of contacting marginalised communities in an area | Tutor Prompt Sheet 21<br>Case studies 1 and 2 | |
| 0.55 | Planning a campaign | Part 1 – Whole group – exercise on how to go about persuading people to join an issue based campaign | Tutor Prompt Sheet 22 | |
| 1.10 | Why should we participate? | Part 2 – Small groups to take on role of one of the groups approached above and think through if they would want to participate in the campaign.<br>Feedback and summary | Tutor Prompt Sheet 22<br>Flipchart relevant questions | |
| 1.50 | Ending game;<br>give back journals | | | |
| 2.00 | End | | | |

# Making contact

In the introduction to this exercise the following points need to be emphasised:

◆ The importance of networking to make contacts

◆ The need to understand and respect other people's interests and agendas

◆ You need to be clear about what you are trying to achieve and why; what are you offering to marginalised communities?

◆ That it is not enough to say – 'We are here and open to everyone; it's their fault if they don't come along.'

◆ That it is important to look at how to reach out to people and communities – different approaches may be needed with each community; as what works for one may not work for others

◆ That thinking ahead about possible barriers will help them to be more effective in their plan

◆ That they need to be creative and to think of interesting and innovative ways to reach out to people – examples can be sharing food sessions, speak easies, events which bring people together, making videos, using community broadcasting ...

There are two case studies for the small groups to work on with questions.

# Involving marginalised communities

You are members of the New Deal for Communities (NDC) Board for an inner city area of a city. The area has a wealth of people from diverse cultural backgrounds, most of them have been living in the area for many years. It is an area that has been identified as having high levels of social and economic deprivation – that's why a successful bid was made for NDC funding.

You know that many of the smaller communities are not currently involved in the NDC project and that they need to be to meet your targets. You have funding to pay for community development workers or to use in other ways to engage and involve all of the communities in the area.

**Decide how you would plan, as the Board, to ensure that all of the communities were contacted and given real opportunities to become involved. What responses might you anticipate arising, and what barriers would you need to be aware of?**

# Involving marginalised communities

You are members of the committee which runs a local community centre. The centre serves an area on the edge of a large town. It is quite a mixed area with some new private estates, older ex-council houses which have been bought by the people who lived there for quite some time, and some low-rise blocks of maisonettes which are controlled by a housing association. More recently, small communities of people from Eastern Europe have arrived and have now settled, having received the right to stay in the UK.

You are aware that only a certain section of the community uses the centre and you want to open up the centre to more people. Otherwise you fear that the grant aid will be cut in the future – and there is an opportunity to obtain the help of a community development worker.

**Decide how you would plan, as the committee, to ensure that all of the communities were contacted and given real opportunities to become involved. What responses might you anticipate arising, and what barriers would you need to be aware of.**

# Joining a campaign

## Part 1

**A whole group exercise on how to go about persuading people to join an issue based campaign.**

Choose a topical subject – examples could be:

◆ How to get the British National Party (BNP) out of your area

◆ How to stop the road widening scheme affecting your area or about speed restrictions

◆ How to get the local chemical firm to stop polluting the local river and the air

◆ Providing a centre for asylum seekers and refugees.

Facilitate a whole group discussion on how they would go about getting support for a campaign.

A structure could be:

1. What would their objectives be – how would they get agreement and clarity on this?

2. Who could they network with? Who do they know?

3. Who else would they want to involve? How could they make contact with them?

The reason this is suggested as a whole group exercise is to enable you to take some control over the comments that might be raised during discussions about such topics; there may be a fair bit of challenging to be done.

Once the outline of a campaign is produced then you can move onto the next small group exercise.

# Part 2

Organise small groups and then give each of them the role of one of the groups it was agreed to approach in the whole group plan. Ask them to think through:

◆ If they would want to participate in the campaign

◆ What are the pros and cons.

For example:

◆ What are the implications for their safety and well being and their existing work? (Why should a Lesbian Gay and Bisexual (LGB) group join a campaign against BNP – what are the personal safety issues for the people involved? Why would Disabled people who rely on their cars for transport want roads blocked?)

◆ Would their group remain marginalised?

◆ What would be the power of their own group within any campaign group; are they just tokens?

◆ Issues of resources?

◆ Do they want others to speak for them?

◆ Is it an opportunity to engage and be recognised?

Flip chart the relevant questions.

# Reflective Journal

*To be completed after each 4 hours of group work*

Name of participant _____

Name of Tutor/s _____

**1** Give a brief description of the topics covered by the group work and highlight your main areas of learning.

**2** What did you think and feel about the group? What did you contribute to the group and its work?

**3** Did you find anything difficult in the session and/or are there areas you would like us to cover again?

## Portfolio question

**You need to explain what you mean by inclusion and exclusion in respect of communities.**

*For level 1* You should give two examples of how people can be excluded from community activities. Then you should explain how a community group/network can take steps to include people.

*For level 2* You should discuss the issues of inclusion and exclusion which affect your community. You should describe how a community group can be enabled to work more inclusively.

*(Complete during the week)*

Make notes of anything or thoughts that have occurred during the week which you feel challenged you, or re-emphasised your beliefs/experiences.

Tutor's comments

Signature of participant _____

Signature of tutor/s _____ Date _____

# Planning and prioritising

# Planning and prioritising
# Session Plan 9 and 10

◆ **Target audience**

Community activists; people working with communities

◆ **Length of session**

2 x 2-hour sessions; four hours in total

◆ **Session aim(s)**

● To enable participants to develop a plan for a community development activity/project.

◆ **Session outcomes**

At the end of the session students/trainees will…

● Demonstrate an understanding of the importance of planning and prioritising in community groups.

◆ **Indicative content**

● Deciding on what to do; methods and approaches to involving people

● Reflecting on what has happened in the past to them and others – lessons they can draw on to help with their planning

● Setting priorities which involve all parts of their communities

● Action planning and planning skills and techniques

● Evaluation and its role and purpose in helping to replan and prioritise.

# Detailed Session Plan 9

| Time | Content | Exercise/Method | Resources | Notes core topic or optional if time |
|------|---------|-----------------|-----------|---------------------------------------|
| 0.00 | Welcome and admin | | | |
| 0.05 | Warm-up game | | | |
| 0.15 | Aim of the session | Tutor input | Tutor Prompt Sheet 23 | |
| 0.20 | Learning from our past | In pairs discuss examples of being involved in community activities that worked well and didn't work well. Put post-it notes on to two flipcharts | Tutor Prompt Sheet 23 Flipchart (2 columns) | |
| 0.40 | Developing the ideas into action (1) | Tutor input on different techniques to use when bringing people together to prioritise actions. Case studies of issues that could come out of a community profile. Small groups to plan for a public event to bring together relevant people | Tutor Prompt Sheet 24 Handout 10 and 11 Handout 12 Case studies 1, 2, 3, 4 | |
| 1.10 | Developing the ideas into action (2) | Tutor input on aims and time line planning. Case study in Section 2. Developing aims and time line planning; coping with changing situations | Tutor Prompt 24 Handout 13-13d Case study task in Section 2 | |
| 1.40 | Feedback | | | |
| 2.00 | End | | | |

# Aim of the session

The next 2 sessions are linked to Key Role C:

◆ Working within communities to select options and make plans for collective action

◆ Contributing to identifying and prioritising a group's needs, opportunities, rights and responsibilities.

The practice principles of working and learning together and participation are particularly relevant to this session.

The aim of these sessions are to enable people to gain skills in working with a group, to prioritise what they want to achieve and make plans that will help them succeed.

In order to begin to use the expertise in the room and demonstrate learning from previous experiences (the basis of reflective action which is needed when reviewing and re-planning), ask people to go into pairs and take two sets of post-it notes (ideally different coloured ones).

Ask them to think of all the community activities or other events they have been involved in that went well and to discuss what made them successful. They should put their ideas onto one set of post-it notes. Then they should think of the activities/events that didn't work so well, and discuss what made them less successful. Ask them to write out their points on the other set of post-it notes.

For the feedback split a flipchart into two columns – one headed 'positive points' and one 'negative points'. Take feedback by asking for similar points from each group, so they can be put together on the flipchart. When both columns are completed; summarise good practice.

*Tutor Prompt Sheet 24*

# Developing the ideas into an action plan

This exercise is the start of work on a case study that runs throughout the day. It follows on from the work on community profiles undertaken on the first day of the course, in the sense that we can assume that a profile has been carried out which has produced agreement on the main issues affecting a community.

The exercise will take participants through a number of stages:

**1** Organising an event to decide on priorities

**2** Developing aims and a time line

**3** Developing an action plan

**4** Evaluating the process.

At each stage you will need to give some input to enable them to complete the next task.

Start by explaining how the day/sessions will follow through a case study. Then organise people into groups to work on a particular case study. As the case studies each have a theme or key target group people may chose which one to work on. The topics are: environmental matters; young people; the town centre; traffic problems. You could put the list on a flip chart and let people sign up or you could read them out.

Once people are in their groups get them to sit so they can hear you. Using Handout 10, introduce some techniques for prioritising ideas. Encourage participants to contribute any other ideas they have come across.

Then give out Handout 12 and talk through the scenario of the small town next to a city where these case studies are set. Get participants to choose their group.

➡

## Task 1 (with Case Studies 1, 2, 3, 4)

The community profile has shown a need to develop services or improve the situation of a certain group of people; several suggestions were made for what was needed. The group needs to decide how they would take forward an area of work; they need to decide who they would bring together and what techniques they would use to get all their ideas out and then organise them into priorities.

These are all written out as tasks for each group – see case study sheets 1, 2, 3, 4.

Ask groups to complete Section 1 of the case study questions. Set a time limit and then get them back together to feedback their ideas quite quickly at this stage. Then move on to Section 2. This is about turning an agreed priority into a set of aims and developing a time line.

You can introduce the type of techniques used to sort priorities using Handouts 13-13d; explain about short, medium and long-term aims.

## Task 2

In their groups participants should look at Section 2 on the case study sheet, where they are given a priority. Then ask them to come up with short, medium and long-term aims for this scenario. They should develop a time line which will get them to decide what tasks need doing and in what order, so that they can achieve their short-term aims and set the scene for longer-term aims.

Once they have done this they will ask you for a set of cards which will provide some information about events that are happening which might affect their plans. There are two cards for each case study. They have to decide if they will re-plan or how they will take account of this new information.

Feedback is at the end of the session where they share their ideas and plans.

# Techniques to prioritise ideas

**These are just some ideas. You can create all sorts of interesting ways of engaging with people, just let your imagination run for a while.**

**1** **Community Maps** – have a large map of the area pinned on a wall or laid out on a table. Give people several small post-it notes – as many as required by the question. Give them a specific question – for example which are the three worst 'grot spots' in the area you would like to see cleaned up?

**2** **Speak-outs** – invite everyone to think of one or two things that they want to see change and then let them talk. Record the points they make on a flip chart. When everyone has had their say and all the ideas/concerns have been listed; give people three 'red dots' (or something similar – you can buy sheets of different sticky shapes from stationers). Ask them to put a number 1, 2, 3 on them and to put them against the idea/point on the flip chart that they feel are the most important.

**3** **The disagree game** – see Handout 11 attached to this sheet for details – you will need small cards or squares of paper with 'I DISAGREE' on one side and blank on the other.

**4** **Building bricks** – cut out brick shaped pieces of paper and give everyone several bricks. Ask them to think about what would be the building bricks to create a better part of the community – for example what would be the building bricks to make the local park attractive for everyone to use. People fill in an idea on each brick and then the whole group comes together to build the wall from the foundations upwards. So, having an accessible entrance might be a foundation, a park ranger on site might be higher up in the wall.

This exercise can be used in the reverse way – ask what are all the obstacles we face trying to get the park usable by everyone, and then you build the wall and work out how to demolish the wall.

# Setting Priorities: Disagree game

Val Harris

## Introduction

The aim of this exercise is to enable a group to decide on its priorities over a period of time, and to establish an action plan. It aims to give everyone an opportunity to contribute their ideas and comments, not just those who are good at talking in groups. It requires some level of literacy, but could be adapted to symbol language without too much difficulty.

## How to do it

You will need several pieces of paper, approximately 2" by 3", with 'I DISAGREE' printed on one side: an A4 sheet of paper can be ruled to give 8–10 rectangles, written on, and then copied. Everyone in the group has several of these pieces of paper, and a pen or pencil.

Ask each member of the group to write down what they think their group should be doing in the next year (or so many months) – each idea on a separate piece of paper. The more pieces of paper people have, the longer the exercise will take, so you could limit it to, say, four main ideas if you want a quicker exercise.

When everyone has finished writing down their ideas, ask them to gather round a table. Make sure that everyone is at the same height – i.e. all standing or all sitting. On the table you will have placed the numbers 1, 2, 3 spread out down one side. These can represent either priorities or time scales (for example what we should start doing now, in 3 months, in 6 months time); make sure it is clear what the numbers represent.

Everyone puts their pieces of paper upside down on the table, they are shuffled, and everyone takes some (not their own) and places them on the table under the priority/timescale of their choice.

It is still an individual choice at this point, and no-one touches the papers laid down by other people. Once all the slips are laid out everyone goes round the table and if they disagree with the priority given to any idea, or they do not understand it, they turn it over so that I DISAGREE shows.

All of the suggestions which are left facing upwards will be transferred to flipcharts and form the basis of an action plan. Only those turned over will be debated, so it is important to make sure that everyone is happy with the position and content of those left unturned.

Pick up all those that have been agreed with in the first section, and write them up as a list on a flipchart, leaving space for an 'Action' column. Then ask a group member to turn over one that has been disagreed with in the first section, and invite bids and comments.

The idea is not to get into a long debate, but to quickly check out if anyone wants clarification about what it means, and then to ask where it should be moved to – the majority view wins! It may remain where it is, move to 2 or 3, or be scrapped.

If the issue looks set to lead to a major discussion, put it to one side and come back to it later to decide how and when the discussion can be held. The idea is to see where quick consensus or majority decisions can be made, so keep the group moving on to the next one, and then the next. As decisions are made, so the items are added to the flipcharts for each priority.

Work through each priority in turn and record all the decisions. After a break the group comes back together, works through the flipcharted lists and agrees what action will be taken, by whom, when, and how; for example it will be put on the next team meeting agenda; it will be brought to the management team's attention; two or three people will take on the task, etc.

The actual exercise should take 30–40 minutes. The discussion of action points will depend on the length of the lists, but again should be fairly quick – at this stage it's about making decisions rather than holding debates.

*This idea was gathered from a workshop on*
*'Action for Neighbourhood Change'*
*run by Tony Gibson at Nottingham University.*

# Developing the ideas into an action plan: using case studies

You live in a small town which is near to a city. It was an independent town before local government changes in the 1970s incorporated it into the city boundary. It has its own town hall and a small shopping centre with an open-air market right in the centre. There are houses and flats in the centre and it is surrounded by streets of Victorian houses, council maisonettes, housing association flats and a few houses build throughout the 20th century. There is a big supermarket just on the edge of the town centre.

You live in the area very near to the town centre. It takes 10 minutes to walk to the central square where the market is held and the buses come and go. A community profile of your community had been undertaken earlier in the year and it had highlighted a number of concerns that people have and want to see some action taken on.

A number of working groups have been set up to take forward different issues and to produce an action plan.

You can join one of the working groups as either a member of the community or someone who gets paid to work in that community.

The working groups are:

**1** Environmental matters

**2** Young people

**3** The town centre

**4** Traffic problems.

Decide which group you want to join and meet up with the others in your group.

# Environmental matters

In the profile a number of matters have been raised including

◆ The state of the alleyways which provided useful short cuts to bus stops and shops

◆ The apparent running down of the local allotments and the level of vandalism to the allotments

◆ The mess around the recycling bins in the car park

◆ The damage done to the new trees planted in the park.

## Section 1

Your working group has to decide how you will follow up on these issues.

Your first task is to agree on some kind of event which will bring together the relevant people to set out the priorities.

**1** *Who will you want to invite to a prioritising and planning event?*

**2** *What sort of event will you organise? What technique will you use to get known everyone's ideas on the environmental matters affecting the community and then to make a list of priorities?*

## Section 2

The priority that was agreed after your public event was to get the mess around the recycling bins in the local car park tidied up.

The reason for this was that it was felt important to show local people that something could happen. Hopefully this would then encourage them to get more involved in other environmental matters.

The car park is on council land which has recently become a short-stay car park. There are skips and bins for paper, cans, plastic bottles, fabrics and shoes, all of which are emptied by different firms. It is next door to the supermarket to which people come from a wide area. They bring their boxes and bags of material to be recycled. The bins quickly fill up, especially at weekends. So people just leave their boxes and bags all around the bins rather than taking them home again. The rubbish blows all over the car park and into people's gardens.

In your group you should make a plan which covers the short, medium and long-term aims of the campaign.

Then you should produce a time line of all the tasks that are needed to achieve the short-term aims and set the scene for the longer-term aims.

When you have made your plan you should ask the tutor for the cards relating to your working group. You should read the cards and then decide what difference it will make to your plan, if any.

# Cards for the environmental group

**1** *When you contact the firms to find out why they are not collecting regularly enough they say that they often send their lorries round but since the council made it a short stay car park with charges, people now double park on the road. The lorries cannot get into the car park to empty the skips, so they have to go away.*

**2** *Your group has a meeting arranged with the Manager of the local supermarket and it has taken ages to organise. The group then gets to hear about a meeting that the council has called about bringing in a paper recycling scheme for the local area. It is at the same time as the meeting with the Manager of the supermarket.*

# Young people

In the profile a number of matters have been raised including:

◆ The number of young people aged 12–15 who hang around in large groups near to the sheltered dwelling complex

◆ The closure of the local youth centre

◆ The young people who skateboard in the car park of the supermarket in the evenings

◆ Homeless young people who sleep in the allotment sheds during the winter months and often beg in the shopping centre.

## Section 1

Your working group has to decide how you will follow up on these issues.

Your first task is to agree on some kind of event which will bring together the relevant people to set out the priorities.

**1** *Who will you want to invite to a prioritising and planning event?*

**2** *What sort of event will you organise? What technique will you use to get known everyone's ideas on the issues around young people in the community and then to make a list of priorities?*

## Section 2

The priority that was agreed after your public event was to bring young people together to get them to decide what provisions they wanted and would use.

The reason for this was that at the public event there had been many different ideas suggested but there was no overall agreement. It was unclear how many people would actually use the different facilities if they were set up. The age range of young people contacted was quite wide, from 12–18. Some of the young people had said that they wanted to learn to run their own groups and plan their own activities.

The council has a youth service which has a team of detached youth workers who can be allocated to different areas to work with local groups. One of them came to the public event and expressed some interest in working in the area.

In your group you should make a plan which covers short, medium and long-term aims of this work. Then you should produce a time line of all the tasks that are needed to achieve the short-term aims and set the scene for the longer-term aims.

When you have made your plan you should ask the tutor for the cards relating to your working group. You should read the cards and then decide what difference it will make to your plan if any.

## Cards for the youth group

**1** *The council announces plans to cut jobs in the youth service, mainly by getting rid of the detached team of workers. They call a public meeting to start a campaign to save their team and its work and ask you to come along. It is at the same time as a meeting you have arranged between the residents of the sheltered housing and some local young people, to talk about their concerns.*

**2** *A scout group which has been meeting for years in the local church hall contacts your group to say its leader is retiring and it will close unless they can get a new leader. They want you to help them find a new leader and to encourage local young people to go to the group.*

# The town centre

In the profile a number of matters have been raised including:

◆ The damage done to the flower beds and seats on Friday and Saturday nights

◆ The run-down look of the outdoor market stalls (market runs Friday, Saturday, Monday)

◆ The lack of information about the buses – which stop and what times the buses run from

◆ The litter created by the take-away shops.

## Section 1

Your working group has to decide how you will follow up on these issues.

Your first task is to agree on some kind of event which will bring together the relevant people to set out the priorities.

**1** *Who will you want to invite to a prioritising and planning event?*

**2** *What sort of event will you organise? What technique will you use to get known everyone's ideas on the problems within the town centre which are affecting the community, and then to make a list of priorities?*

## Section 2

The priority that was agreed after your public event was to raise the profile of the town centre and to get the council and others to focus on its needs. This would be done through a two day fun event in the town square. The event would launch an initiative to get the people who live and work in the town centre involved in developing a longer-term action plan. It would also show that people did care about their town centre.

This priority was chosen as people felt that the town was slowly running down as local shops closed while the supermarket expanded and more charity shops moved into the shopping area. Action was needed now to reverse the decline and make the town attractive to people. A fun way of involving local people and businesses would also bring about publicity for the town and encourage others to join in.

In your group you should make a plan which covers short, medium and long-term aims of the campaign. Then you should produce a time line of all the tasks that are needed to achieve the short-term aims and set the scene for the longer-term aims.

When you have made your plan you should ask the tutor for the cards relating to your working group. You should read the cards and then decide what difference it will make to your plan, if any.

# Cards for the town centre group

**1** *You have got your plan together for the event in a few weeks time when the stall holders from the open market approach you and say they have been told that the council is thinking of getting rid of the outdoor market and making it into a car park. The market is really important in bringing people into the town centre. They ask for your support.*

**2** *You have done all the planning for the event and the publicity is ready to go. The date is in many people's diaries and has been widely talked about. The police contact you to say that they can no longer offer police cover as they have a football match in the nearby city to cover and they want you to change the date.*

# Traffic

In the profile a number of matters have been raised including:

◆ The traffic congestion created by people bringing their children to the local primary school

◆ The 24-hour opening of the local supermarket has led to more traffic on nearby streets

◆ The double parking on some roads now that the car parks are charging for all-day parking

◆ The fear of more traffic coming through the area once the relief road for the next town is completed and open.

## Section 1

Your working group has to decide how you will follow up on these issues.

Your first task is to agree on some kind of event which will bring together the relevant people to set out the priorities.

**1** *Who will you want to invite to a prioritising and planning event?*

**2** *What sort of event will you organise? What technique will you use to get known everyone's ideas on the traffic problems affecting the community and then to make a list of priorities?*

# Section 2

The priority that was agreed after your public event was to get traffic calming and a resident parking scheme for the area.

The reason for this was that the roads are congested by the cars of people who work in the town parking on the streets all day. They park there to avoid paying the car park charges recently brought in by the council to deal with the congestion right in the town centre which was affecting businesses and delivery lorries. This makes it difficult for local people to come and go during the day, especially for older and Disabled people who cannot get anywhere near their homes to park after going out to the doctor's or shopping. The streets near to the school are also used as rat-runs by motorists going into the city to avoid waiting at the traffic lights at a busy junction.

In your group you should make a plan which covers short, medium and long-term aims of the campaign. Then you should produce a time line of the all tasks that are needed to achieve the short-term aims and set the scene for the longer-term aims.

When you have made your plan you should ask the trainer for the cards relating to your working group. You should read the cards and then decide what difference it will make to your plan, if any.

# Cards for the traffic group

**1** *You read in the local paper that the council is going to cut its budget for traffic calming measures in residential areas as it forgot to apply to the central government in time for this money for the coming year. There is a full council meeting next week to agree this budget cut.*

**2** *The supermarket manager, who is attending a local area meeting about the town centre, announces that they will oppose any traffic calming measures that they think might put people off coming to the store.*

# Starting to develop a plan

When you are beginning to plan an event or a campaign there are five points that are important:

**1** That you are sure as a group what your aims are – these should be clear, straightforward and easy to measure so you know when you have achieved them

**2** That you split your aims into short, medium and longer-term (as appropriate) so as not to put people off by having long lists which are very daunting

**3** That you are aware of the resources that you will need, and what you have available to you. How much time and energy does your group have? What will it need? What money will you need? What about other resources?

**4** That you put the plan into a time frame – so that it is clear what needs doing now and what later

**5** That you set a review date so you can see where you have got to and what needs to change.

There are different ways that your group can work together to make the overall plan. They all work best using post-it notes so they can be moved around as your group discusses them.

# Fish Bones

This technique provides a framework for getting all the issues into manageable groupings.

Put the subject in the bubble and then think of all of the possible issues/ways of doing things and put them on post-its. Through discussion, group them into the main categories on the fish bones.

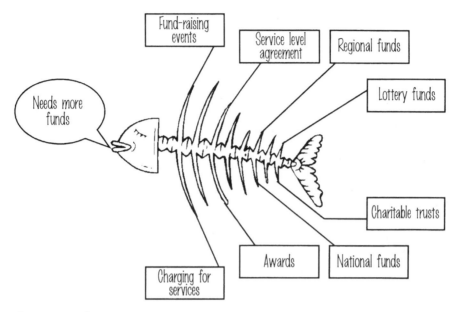

# Mind Mapping

One way of getting all your ideas on a particular topic arranged in a more detailed way is to structure the different bits using a mind map. Put the topic in the centre and then write the key issues in the bubbles nearest to the centre and then add in all the associated ideas in the surrounding bubbles.

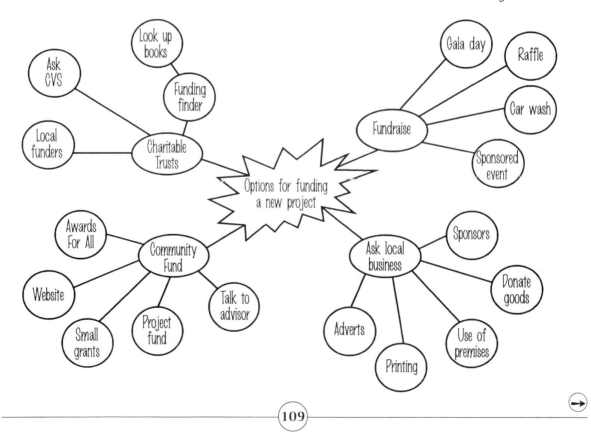

# Tree Diagrams

This technique aims to break down an issue into various parts. You start by identifying the issue/problem and write it in the box on the left hand side. Ask the group how the issue/problem can be resolved and keep asking "how" until practical ideas emerge.

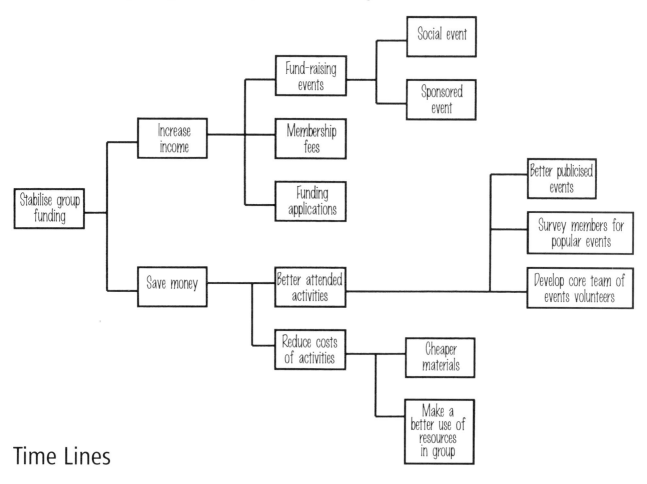

# Time Lines

All the tasks are written out on post-it notes and then put into the order they need to be carried out in. There are different categories of time line you can use, for example:

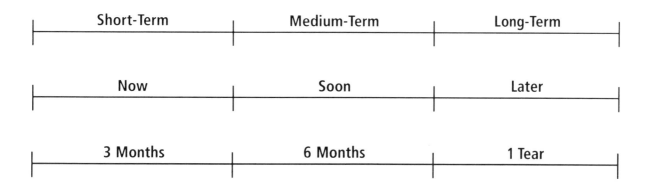

*See next sheet for a worked example of a time line.*

# Time Line Example: Raise £1000 for a new project's running costs and buy a new photocopier

Time line showing tasks positioned along a scale from 0, 3 months, 6 months, 1 year, grouped under Short Term, Medium Term, Long Term.

**Short Term**

Raise £1000 for project:
- **What:** – Apply to Awards For All for pack
  **Who:** – Joy
  **When:** – 27th June
- **What:** – Prepare budgets
  **Who:** – Jannine
  **When:** – 3rd July
- **What:** – Complete form
  **Who:** – Shazia/Tom
  **When:** – Next committee meeting. End July

New photocopier:
- **What:** – Check web for recycled photocopiers
  **Who:** – Zaira
  **When:** – Beginning August
- **What:** – Second-hand donated machine from xxx firm
  **Who:** – Mark
  **When:** – Beginning September

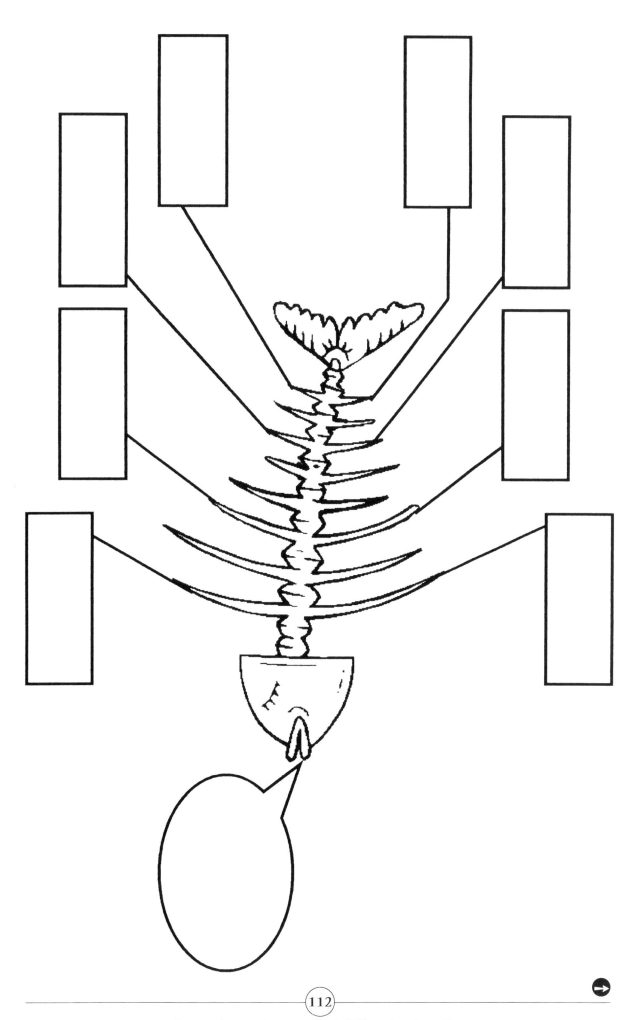

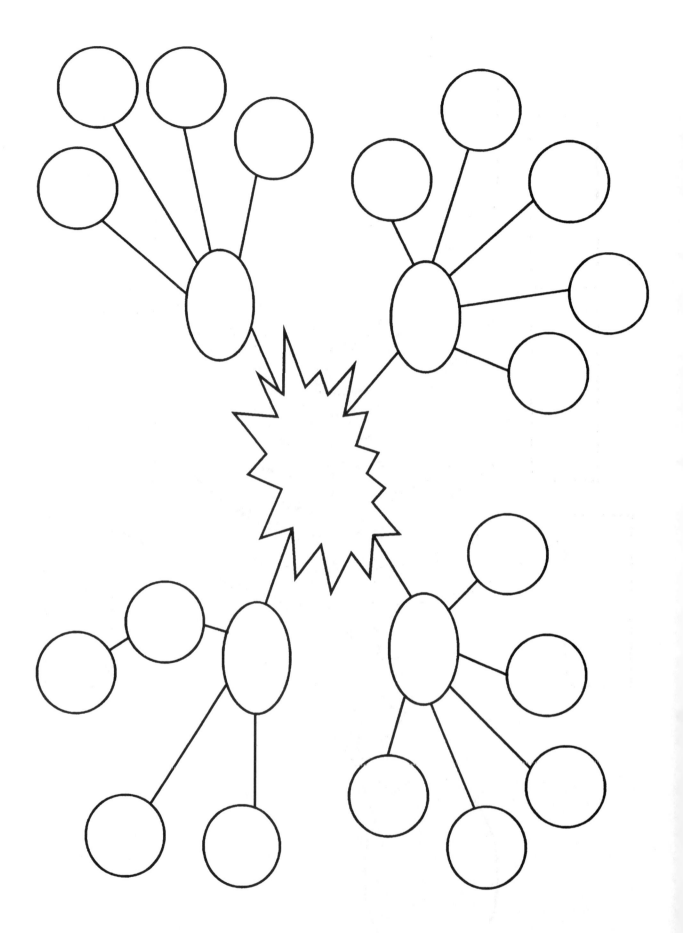

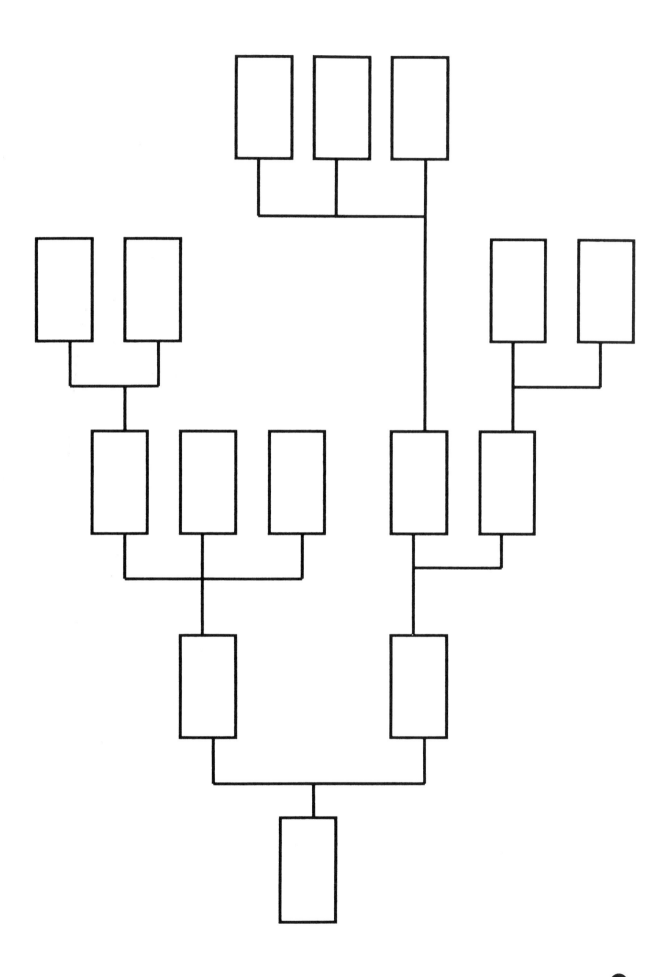

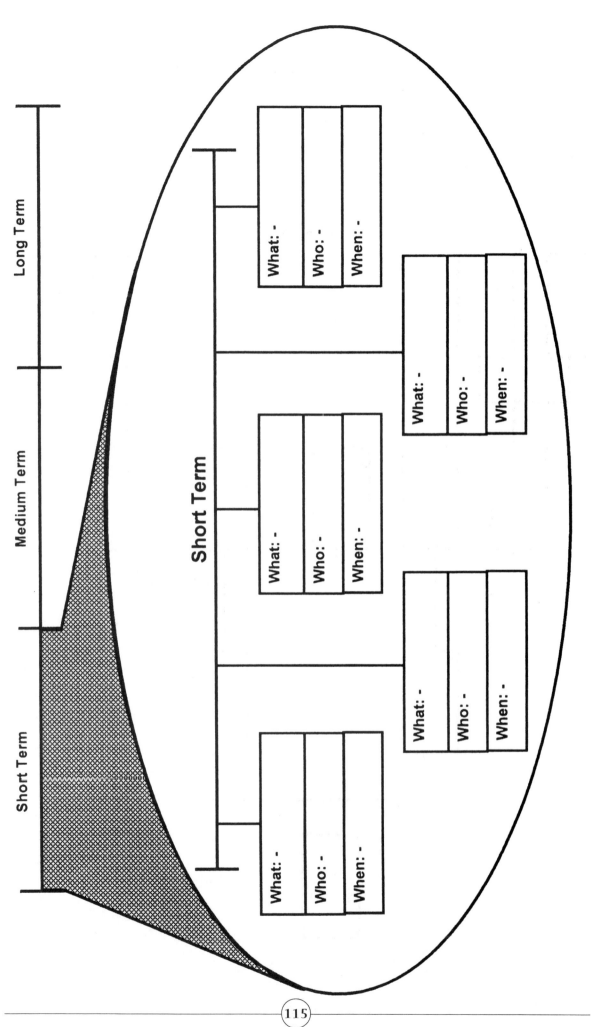

# Detailed Session Plan 10

| Time | Content | Exercise/Method | Resources | Notes *core topic or optional if time* |
|------|---------|-----------------|-----------|-------|
| 0.00 | Wake-up game | | | |
| 0.10 | Developing the ideas into action (3) | Tutor input on action planning Case study section 3. | Tutor Prompt Sheet 25 Handout 14: Case study – task 3 to produce an action plan based on time line and aims agreed before | |
| | | Feedback from all groups | | |
| 1.10 | Evaluation of the process | The value of evaluation and review in the planning process – Tutor input. Small groups to decide how and when to include in their plan. What criteria would they use for success? What and how would they gather information? | Tutor Prompt Sheet 26 with Handout 15. Handout 16: Case study – part 4 | |
| 1.50 | Ending game; give back journals | | | |
| 2.00 | End | | | |

Community Development Work Skills • **Session Ten**
*Federation for Community Development Learning*

# Action planning

**This exercise continues from Session 9 with the same case studies they worked on previously. The same groups reconvene and their task no.3 is to produce an action plan sheet.**

You introduce the proforma for action planning, and talk through the headings. It is important to stress that plans only work if they are broken down into bite sized tasks that people can do, and know how to do. Action plans that are long on rhetoric are not worth writing. All action plans need to have names and dates by each task.

In their groups they should use the points from their overall plan and produce an action plan in the format of the sheet.

# Case study – part 3

You are going to produce an action plan to achieve the short-term aims of your project. Using the work you have already produced on your aims and the time line make an action plan using the headings in the table provided overleaf.

## Action Plans

Once the timetable has been agreed, it is important that all tasks are completed on schedule and that the group co-ordinates its activities.

A good way of achieving these outcomes is to produce an agreed action plan for each project to be undertaken. This involves splitting the work into specific tasks with one or two people who take lead responsibility for getting the task done by an agreed date. An example of an action plan could look like the following:

| Activity/ Task | People responsible | People who can help | By when | Review date |
|---|---|---|---|---|
| | | | | |

Action plans carefully drawn up in consultation with all the people involved have a number of advantages:

◆ They help to identify the work to be done

◆ They clarify everyone's roles

◆ They focus on completion dates

◆ They provide a common sense of ownership and teamwork

Action Plan

Name(s):

Project:

| Activity/Task | People responsible | People who can help | By when | Review date |
|---|---|---|---|---|
| | | | | |
| | | | | |
| | | | | |
| | | | | |
| | | | | |
| | | | | |
| | | | | |

# Evaluating the process

**This is the final part of the exercise on planning and prioritising. It is about evaluating the process and the progress of the plan.**

Refer back to the learning cycle and the reflective practitioner role of community development. Introduce the need for all plans to be regularly reviewed – both to see what progress has been made and what needs to change, and to learn from the process they chose to see whether it was the best they could do and what they might do differently in future.

In their case study groups they need to decide how and when they would:

**1** Review the progress of the plan

**2** Review the process they used and to see what they would do differently next time.

The technique is an adaptation of the look back and move forward kit available from Shell Better Britain Campaign, www.sbbc.co.uk/lbmf

Give out Handout 15.

# Looking back to see how to move forwards

**There are many variations of this technique; this one is adapted from the 'look back move forward' exercise that Shell Better Britain has produced (more details www.sbbc.co.uk/lbmf )**

Make a large wall poster (using flipcharts stuck together or a roll of wallpaper), with three horizontal lines running along it (see diagram below)

At the bottom you write out your original time line and action points.

Give everyone who is involved in this review lots of post-it notes and ask them to think about the highs and lows over the past xx number of months that the group is reviewing. People put the high on the top half and the lows underneath.

When everyone has put up their ideas, gather people so they can see the wall chart and read out the post-it notes around each event or time period. Discuss each section and on a separate flipchart make a note of all the points that emerge; what the group has learnt and what it would do differently next time.

| Name of group | Date of review |
|---|---|
| | |
| *Highs* | |
| | |
| *Lows* | |
| | |

Case study part 4

# Reviewing progress and the process

**This is the final part of this exercise.**

## Reviewing progress

As a group you have your plan; you need to review it at regular intervals to make sure the group are on track or to make changes if needed.

**1** *Agree the timescale for reviewing the plan*

**2** *Looking back at your aims – what would you accept as success for each of them?*

**3** *What information would you need to know if you had succeeded or not?*

**4** *Who could give you this information?*

**5** *How would you carry out a review of the progress of the plan?*

## Reviewing the process

You selected different techniques as you went through the simulation. How would you find out if they were the best choices, or if there were lessons that could be used to refine the techniques for future use or to develop different techniques? Who would you involve?

# Reflective Journal

*To be completed after each 4 hours of group work*

---

Name of participant _____

Name of Tutor/s _____

---

**1** Give a brief description of the topics covered by the group work and highlight your main areas of learning.

**2** What did you think and feel about the group? What did you contribute to the group and its work?

**3** Did you find anything difficult in the session and/or are there areas you would like us to cover again?

# Portfolio question

**For level 1** You should describe at least two ways of getting a group to prioritise their work and explain the techniques. Explain how you think you could get your community group, or one you know about, to produce its own plan.

**For level 2** You need to explain why it is important for community groups to plan their activities, give some examples. Describe how a group could be encouraged/enabled to produce a plan for its activities.

*(Complete during the week)*

Make notes of anything or thoughts that have occurred during the week which you feel challenged you, or re-emphasised your beliefs/experiences.

Tutor's comments

Signature of participant _____

Signature of tutor/s _____ Date _____

# Resources to support community development

# Resources to support community development
## Session Plan 11 and 12

◆ **Target audience**

Community activists; people working with communities

◆ **Length of session**

2 x 2-hour sessions; four hours in total

◆ **Session aim(s)**

● To examine the range of resources available for community development activities.

◆ **Session outcomes**

At the end of the session students/trainees will…

● Demonstrate an understanding of the resources available to support community development activities.

◆ **Indicative content**

● Identifying the resources communities/groups needs

● Identifying different sources of resources

● Making use of resources within the community and available to it

● Getting resources

● Sustainability and environmental issues related to resources.

# Detailed Session Plan 11

| Time | Content | Exercise/Method | Resources | Notes *core topic or optional if time* |
|------|---------|-----------------|-----------|--------|
| 0.00 | Welcome and warm-up game | | | |
| 0.10 | Explain the admin and arrangements for the ending of the course<br><br>Aims of today | Tutor input<br><br>Tutor input – aims link to Key Role E | Any Open College Network forms<br><br>Tutor Prompt Sheet 27 | |
| 0.20 | Resources for a new group | Exercise in small groups to make checklist of the resources needed | Handout 17<br>Tutor Prompt Sheet 28 | |
| 0.40 | Resources within the group | Exercise in same group to develop a skills audit | Handout 18<br>Tutor Prompt Sheet 28 | |
| 1.10 | External resources | Exercise in same group to complete sheet on resources needed and where to get them | Handout 19<br>Tutor Prompt Sheet 28 | |
| 1.30 | Network maps | Exercise in small groups to draw map to see what resources group can access | Handout 20<br>Tutor Prompt Sheet 28 | |
| 1.50 | Display of maps | Pin on walls for people to look at | | |
| 2.00 | End | | | |

# Aim of session 11

**The final key role that is examined in this introduction to community development work skills is about making the best use of resources. Key role E requires people to encourage the best use of resources – by contributing both to the planning, use and monitoring of resources.**

Community development workers need to know the range of resources available to their groups and networks and how to access them. They also need to develop skills in making decisions about whether or not to accept proffered resources and to explore the conditions attached to them.

# Resources

**The exercise on resources runs through until the middle of session 12. Organise people into small groups – ideally of four – and they will work in this group all of this session.**

## Task

The scenario is laid out in Handout 17; the aim of this exercise is to get the groups to appreciate the full range of resources available for community development.

They are asked to put together all their ideas about resources they will need to set up a new group to tackle the low level of basic and key skills in their community.

Take the feedback and group the post-it notes into different kinds of resources, such as people, finance, equipment, premises etc.

This list will be left visible during the session so they can use it as a checklist.

## Task

Handout 18 takes the scenario onto the next stage; where a group of people have come together and they need to find out what resources are within the group.

Their task is the decide what information they need about the group's members and how they would go about undertaking a skills audit of the group.

You could introduce some ideas when you set the exercise – such as making a little questionnaire for people to fill in; people to interview other members of a group with a checklist; versions of people bingo with skills needed in the squares.

In the feedback they should explain why they decided to take their agreed approach.

## Task

Handout 19 is about the group finding out what external resources are available to them using the prepared grid .

## Task

This is the last exercise for this session (Handout 20). The aim is to get the participants to think about how they could use their contacts to get hold of resources. The exercise gets the groups to make network maps. The feedback is through them displaying their maps to each other.

# To establish the resources needed to set up a new group

The English Government, through its Neighbourhood Renewal Unit, has issued a discussion paper called the Learning Curve. It is all about the involvement of communities in regeneration and renewal programmes. One issue that it mentions is the low level of basic skills (meaning literacy, numeracy) and key skills (such as IT, problem solving, communication, problem solving and working with others) of people in the most disadvantaged and deprived area. The paper suggests that the low level of skills stops people getting jobs.

Your local partnership board has read the document and wants to set up a project in the community which would tackle the lack of basic and key skills through involving people in community groups and community activities.

It has asked you, as the community development worker for the area, to set up a new group which will involve all the sections of the community which can take this idea forward. The group will become a formal group attached to the partnership, although the precise nature of the relationship has yet to be worked out.

**Your first task is to make a checklist of all the resources you will need to get this group formed and ready to undertake work on this project.**

By resources we can mean:

◆   People – local people with their skills, knowledge, time, energy, contacts

◆   Experts/professionals who have specialist expertise

◆   Money

◆   Support in kind – such as access to telephones, photocopiers, seconded staff

◆   Premises – somewhere to work from

◆   Equipment – computers, books, etc.

**Put all your ideas on post-it notes and group them together into different kinds of resources ready for the feedback from all the small groups.**

# Finding out about the resources within the group

As community development workers you have been successful in getting many people from different sections of the community to agree to join the new group. The group will take forward this project on improving people's basic and key skills through community based activities and provision.

Your next task is to find out more about the people who have come along and what resources they can bring to the project. They are a real mixed group:

◆ Some live in the area

◆ Some work there

◆ Some say they are just local mums and dads

◆ Others say they are basic skills tutors from the nearby college

◆ Some seem to have a lot to say – although it is not always relevant – and others are quite quiet but seem to be taking it all in.

**You need to devise a suitable skills audit which will give you the information you need.**

**1** *Work out what information you want – make a list*

**2** *Work out the best way(s) to get this information – explain how you would do this*

**3** *Explain your reasons for taking this approach.*

# External resources

Once you have undertaken your skills audit within the group you will know what resources you have available to you. You now need to think about what gaps there are between what you have and what you know you will need.

**Make a list of all the external resources you need and your initial thoughts on where you might go to get these resources.**

| *Resources* | *Where to get them* |
|---|---|
| 1. | |
| 2. | |
| 3. | |
| 4. | |
| 5. | |

Community Development Work Skills • **Session Eleven**
*Federation for Community Development Learning*

# Network maps

**One way to find out where resources are and how to access them is to share your ideas and contacts. You can do this by making a 'map' or diagram of who you know.**

In your group, sit around a large piece of paper and take one side/end of the paper. Draw a small picture of yourself, and then begin to add around you people you know – so you draw a small line to any family who live nearby, then you draw lines from them to who they might know.

You can have another line to people you know from work, or from any group you attend. If you draw the same people as the other people in your group – start to link them up.

Your tutor will show you how this is done.

As you put people onto the 'map' discuss amongst yourselves what resources they may have that can help your group.

By the end of this exercise you should have a good idea of where to go to get resources and who can help you get them.

# Detailed Session Plan 12

| Time | Content | Exercise/Method | Resources | Notes *core topic or optional if time* |
|------|---------|-----------------|-----------|-------|
| 0.00 | Wake-up game | | | |
| 0.15 | Deciding about proffered resources | Role play<br>Preparation<br>Running<br>Discussion<br>Debriefing | Tutor Prompt Sheet 29, Handout 21 and role sheets cut into seven slips and enough observers slips to give everyone a role | |
| 1.05 | Quiz | In teams; mark each others | Quiz sheets | |
| 1.20 | Course evaluation | | | |
| 1.35 | Last minute admin | | | |
| 1.45 | Ending exercise | Positive posters | Posters | |
| 2.00 | End | | | |

# Making decisions on proffered resources

**The aim of this exercise is to get participants to consider what sort of resources they would accept and under what conditions (Handout 21).**

The scenario continues on from the one used in session 11. The scene is that the group have organised three people to go off and collect information from people/organisations identified in their network maps.

They are now at their next meeting and it is to be run as a role play. You need a chair, three reporters and three committee members; the rest of the group can be additional committee members or observers. The reporters have specific information to bring to the meeting, the committee members have prescribed roles.

Allocate the roles – brief the chair while the others read their roles.

The role play should last about 15–20 minutes. Allow time for discussion in roles and then start the de-briefing by bringing in the observers. Start to talk about the decisions that were made – or not; and record the issues raised by the role play scenario.

# Making a decision on proffered resources

You are at a group meeting. After your last meeting when you drew up your network maps some people had agreed to go and talk to identified key people who might be able to help with external resources and particularly with money. You have been offered quite a lot of help 'in kind' but you need real money to make the project take off.

You have agreed that the project will consist of several small 'self -help' mini projects which will involve people in the community in planning and running their own activities. By doing this they will develop and improve their basic and key skills.

Your ideas are for:

◆ A youth group who want to run an evening drop-in session each week

◆ An Asian women's health and fitness group

◆ A support group for refugee and asylum seekers

◆ A 'reading with your child' project for young parents

◆ A dad's group to run a weekend football league.

This meeting has been called to hear what people have found out and to make decisions on whether you want to take the resources being offered or not.

You will be given a role to take at this meeting either as a reporter or committee member – you should report back as your written brief says. Or you will be asked to be an observer of what is going on in the meeting, to report back at the end of the meeting – so you will need to make notes.

# Role cards

*(To be photocopied and cut out)*

---

## Chair

You need to set the agenda at the start of the meeting and keep order!

There are three reporters who need to make their reports back, and there are three committee members, each with a different brief.

At the end you must sum up the arguments and get the group to try and make decisions.

---

## Reporter 1

You have been to the local college which is about a mile-and-a-half away from the edge of the community. The people you spoke to were very keen on improving people's basic skills as they have a contract to do this work from the local Learning and Skills Council.

They extol the virtues of their open learning centre with all its gleaming computers and videos and books and learning packs. They also told you about the skills of their on-site tutors. They say it's free – well to people who live on certain roads which are their priority area, the others may have to pay. They need to attract people from their priority groups – Black and Minority Ethnic communities, young people who have just left the care system and the over-fifties.

They have an on-site crèche which might have some spaces. Parents would need to book from week to week as the part-time staff are given priority.

Unfortunately they cannot provide community-based provision as they don't have any money for this. They have to use their approved tutors but they can offer day and evening sessions. They can't offer help with travel costs.

## Reporter 2

You have been talking to a member of the new Primary Care Trust (PCT) for your area. They are looking to fund projects that will make a difference to the health of people in their catchment area. They need to meet their government set targets on reducing heart disease, tackling drugs, stopping people smoking, reducing diabetes especially amongst the Asian communities and reducing obesity especially amongst children.

The PCT covers all the doctors' surgeries and clinics in your area but it covers a much wider geographical area. The health issues in other areas may be different so you need to make out a case about why they should fund your projects. The PCTs are new and they are still trying to sort out how they will work and how they will fund community projects. However, in principle they like the idea of community-based projects. They suggest that maybe some could run in their surgeries and clinics. They do have quite a lot of money but only if they meet their targets for improving health.

## Reporter 3

You have been talking to the funding advisor at your local Council for Voluntary Service (CVS). They have explained that it is difficult to get core funding for running the main group but that the partnership has money which it could use for this. It is easier to get smaller amounts of money for different activities. Local businesses, building societies, charitable trust funds may all give money but you will have to fill in forms and check you meet their particular interests. You will need to make several applications as not every one will be successful. This takes time and when you do get the money it requires many different reports to be made on the monies once they have been spent.

## Committee member 1

You are here to listen to what is being said and to try to make sure that the original plan you made as a group is kept to.

## Committee member 2

You just want something to happen and you are not really too bothered about where the money comes from; after all, you can sort it all out later. Once you have the money they can't take it back – can they?

## Committee member 3

You are from the newly forming Refugee and Asylum Seekers' Support Group.

You are worried that the current public and governmental attitude towards refugees and asylum seekers will make it hard to get funding for your group and that you might get cut out of the partnership.

You know that many of the refugees and asylum seekers have many skills. If they could just be helped with their English then they could get jobs once their status had been confirmed.

Community Development Work Skills • **Session Twelve**
*Federation for Community Development Learning*

# Community Development Work Skills Quiz

Quiz
Sheet

Team name:

Team members:

**1** Give three reasons why you would gather information about a community

**2** Give five ways of how you would gather this information. (Point for each)

**3** Name official roles held within a management committee

**4** Give three examples of where power could be held within a group

**5** Outline of the main aspects of the life cycle of a group?

**6** Suggest three ways in which communication can cause problems in a group

**7** Give three examples of how good communication can help a group

**8** What does exclusion mean for a community and for individuals?

**9** Give four examples of people who may be excluded from joining groups

**10** What does inclusion mean?

**11** How can a community group be inclusive? (point for each)

**12** Give one way that a group can prioritise their work?

**13** What are the key elements of an action plan?

**14** Name three resources available to community groups

**15** How can groups access available resources – point for each.

# Reflective Journal

*To be completed after each 4 hours of group work*

Name of participant _____

Name of Tutor/s _____

**1** Give a brief description of the topics covered by the group work and highlight your main areas of learning.

**2** What did you think and feel about the group? What did you contribute to the group and its work?

**3** Did you find anything difficult in the session and/or are there areas you would like us to cover again?

# Portfolio question

**For level 1**  You should give two detailed examples of the support and resources available to your group and to other community groups/networks.

**For level 2**  You should describe the wide range of support and resources available to community groups you know and explain how a group can access them.

*(Complete during the week)*

**Make notes of anything or thoughts that have occurred during the week which you feel challenged you, or re-emphasised your beliefs/experiences.**

Tutor's comments

Signature of participant _____

Signature of tutor/s _____ Date _____